SUNDAY TIMES BESTSELLING AUTHOR

CASEY WATSON

A Last Kiss For Mommy

A teenage mom, a tiny infant,
a terrible choice

To my wonderful and supportive family

This book is a work of non-fiction based on the author's experiences.
In order to protect privacy, names, identifying characteristics,
dialogue and details have been changed or reconstructed.

HarperElement
An imprint of HarperCollins*Publishers*
1 London Bridge Street
London SE1 9GF

www.harpercollins.co.uk

First published by HarperElement 2013
This edition published 2016

1 3 5 7 9 10 8 6 4 2

A catalogue record of this book is
available from the British Library

ISBN 978-0-00-819178-8

Printed and bound in the United States
by RR Donnelley

Acknowledgements

I would like to thank all of the team at HarperCollins, the lovely Andrew Lownie, and my friend and mentor, Lynne.

Chapter 1

I've known my fostering link worker, John Fulshaw, for something approaching seven years now, so I've got to know his face pretty well. I've seen his happy face, his sad face, his 'I don't know how to tell you what I'm about to tell you' face, his concerned face, his angry face and his 'Don't worry, I've got your back' face as well.

So there wasn't much that got past me, and today was no exception. There'd been this glint in his eye since the start of our meeting; a glint that told me that today he was wearing his 'I can't wait to tell you' face. He'd had ants in his pants since he'd arrived.

It was a chilly autumn morning at the end of October. Not quite cold enough to put the heating on mid-morning, but certainly cold enough for me to be wearing my standard winter months outfit of leggings, a fluffy jumper and boots. My husband Mike had taken a rare day off from his job as a warehouse manager, and we were all grouped around the dining table, drinking coffee and trying to avoid eating too many biscuits, because it was the day we had our annual review.

It's something all foster carers have, as a part of what we do – a summing up of how things have gone during the previous year. It's a time to look back to previous placements, discuss what went well and what didn't, talk about any complaints and allegations (none for us, thankfully) and, if appropriate, talk about what new things might happen in the coming year. It's also an opportunity to discuss further training. As specialist foster carers we usually attend at least three training courses per year. In our case, today, everything had been positive, thank goodness. Not every placement works out well – that's the nature of the job – but we had had a good year and Dawn Foster, the reviewing officer, who was also present, had praised me and Mike for the way we'd handled our last placement: two unrelated nine-year-old boys. Both had certainly been in need of support. Jenson was somewhat wayward, being the child of a neglectful single mother – one who'd left him and his sister home alone while going off on holiday with her boyfriend for a week. Georgie's problems were different. He was autistic and had come from a children's home that was closing down; the place where he'd spent almost all of his young life. Individually, both boys came with their own challenges, but our biggest challenge was that we'd had them both together. It had been a rocky ride at times, but, thankfully, they ended up friends.

The review over, and with Dawn on her way back to the office, I closed the front door with a now familiar tingle. We were between placements at the moment and the warm glow I'd felt when Dawn had been singing our praises had now been replaced with a feeling I knew all too well; one of excited anticipation. Just why did John have those ants in his pants? At last I'd have a chance to find out.

When I went back into the dining room – well, dining area, actually; the downstairs of our house is open plan – John was grinning and rubbing his hands together.

'Well?' I asked. Mike looked at me quizzically, but John laughed.

'Get the kettle back on then,' he said, his eyes glinting mischievously, 'and I'll tell you what I've been dying to tell you for the last hour.'

By the time I got back, of course, the pair of them were both grinning like idiots, so it was clear Mike was now one step ahead of me. I set the tray down and took my place back at the dining table. 'Come on then,' I said, plonking both elbows down. 'Spit it out.'

Mike laughed, seeing my expression. 'I think you'd better, John.'

John took his time, picking up his mug and taking a first sip of fresh coffee. 'Actually, it's not so much a "tell" as something I want to run by you.'

Which was always ominous. John had a history of wanting to 'run things by' us. It invariably meant he wasn't confident that it was something we'd say yes to – at least wouldn't say yes to if we had any sense. But that never fazed us. We had never been trained to do mainstream fostering. We were specialists – we specialised in taking the sort of kids that were too damaged or disturbed, for whatever reason, to be suitable for mainstream fostering or adoption.

So what would it be today? I raised my eyebrows enquiringly. 'So, Casey,' John said, speaking mostly to me now. It was me, after all, who'd do the day-to-day childcare. We fostered together but Mike obviously had his full-time job as well.

'Yes,' I said eagerly.

'Well, it's this,' he said. 'Have you ever considered a mother and baby placement?'

I caught my breath. No, I hadn't. It had never even occurred to me. A baby was hardly likely to be damaged at such a tender age, after all. On the other hand, what about the mother? My mind leapt ahead. A baby! I adored babies. Always had. Everyone knew just how besotted I was with my own two grandsons, Levi and Jackson. 'What do you mean, exactly?' I thought to ask then. 'A mother and a baby, or a young pregnant girl?'

John grinned. He could read my expressions just as easily as I could read his. And mine currently had the word 'baby' flashing up in neon on my forehead. He knew how fond I was of saying how much I could almost eat my little grandsons, so it was odds on my interest would be piqued.

'Good point,' he said. 'You've obviously read the handbook very thoroughly, because you're right; a mother and baby placement can be either. But in this case, an actual baby. The mum, Emma, is just fourteen and baby Roman is three weeks old.'

'Oh!' I cooed. 'Roman! What a lovely name she's chosen!' I turned to Mike. 'Oh, please, we must. Oh, imagine having a new baby in the house. It would be great.'

'Slow down, love,' Mike warned, as I'd already known he would. That was the way it worked with us – I was all enthused and optimistic, whereas Mike was more reticent, always considering potential pitfalls. As systems went, it was a good one, because though more often than not I got my way, it at least meant I rushed into things slightly better informed than I would have been if left to my usual impetuous devices.

He turned to John now. 'Did she have the baby in care?' he wanted to know. 'Or is she just coming into the system?'

'Good question,' John said. 'And you're right to be cautious, Mike. Emma has been in and out of care for most of her life. Her mother swings between periods of calm and what seems to be pretty "difficult" behaviour. It's a familiar story, sadly. The mum is alcohol and drug dependent most of the time, and suffers from depression too – cause and effect? – though she does go through periods of drying out now and again. She's a single parent, and Emma is her only child. When she's clean she always wants to have Emma back living with her again – which is what Emma usually wants, too – but it's never too long before the depression takes over again, and then the drinking starts and the poor kid is scooted back into the care of social services quick-smart.'

The atmosphere in the room changed. That was all part of the process; going from asking all about a new child who needed us, to the sober contemplation of just how that state of affairs had come about. The baby, for the moment, was forgotten, as my heart went out to his mother – this poor fourteen-year-old girl who I didn't yet know. I took a moment, even though I knew we would have to take her in. I mustn't let Mike and John think I was jumping in too quickly and not taking time to assess the situation properly. I tried to hide my growing excitement (and it was excitement, no question) as I turned and spoke to John.

'So what's the situation?' I asked. 'Any boy in the background who is willing to take responsibility?'

John reached into his briefcase and took out a by now familiar buff-coloured file. Popping on his reading glasses he then flicked through some pages. 'Yes and no,' he said. 'It's complicated. What happened,' he glanced up, 'well, according to the mother, anyway, is that Emma had started running a bit wild and next thing was that she found herself pregnant. She'd been back living at home again for almost a year by this time – a pretty longish stretch, given the history. Anyway, when the mother found out about the pregnancy she insisted Emma have an abortion, but Emma apparently refused. At that point the mother washed her hands of her completely, and threw her out, apparently thinking that in doing so she might make Emma come to her senses.'

Mike frowned. 'So not out of character at all, then,' he muttered drily. And I tended to agree with him. Could I ever imagine throwing my teenage pregnant daughter out on the street just to make her 'come to her senses'? Not in a million years. I couldn't think of a more perfectly designed recipe for disaster. But then, I wasn't her, was I? And drink, drugs and depression affected a person in all sorts of dangerous ways.

'Well, exactly,' John agreed. 'And of course, the abortion didn't happen, and since that time Emma's been staying with various friends, mostly with another girl – a friend who lives on the same estate, with her single mum. That's where she is now. But since the baby was born just over three weeks ago, the girl's mum's apparently said she can't afford to keep both Emma and Roman, and that's the point when Emma's mum finally got in touch with social services.'

'To put her straight back into care again,' I said. It wasn't a question. Just a sad, all too familiar statement of fact: she obviously didn't want either daughter or grandchild back at home with her, presumably as the lesson hadn't been learned. 'What about the boyfriend, then?' I went on, thinking what a desperate situation it was for a baby to be born into. 'There'd be some police involvement, wouldn't there, given that she's under age?'

John paused to sip some coffee. 'As I say, it's complicated. And here's the stinger; we and just about everyone else, apparently, believe the father is a nineteen-year-old drug dealer, name of Tarim. Emma had been seeing him for some time, it seems, though she has always denied that he's the father.'

'As I suppose she would,' Mike said, 'if she didn't want to get him into trouble.'

John smiled wryly. 'Which he already is. He's in prison right now, doing time for dealing. Went down while she was still pregnant. He has previous form, apparently – so has not been on the scene at all. And though Emma's adamant he's not the father, the woman she's been staying with is absolutely convinced he is. The baby is the spit of him, apparently. Though of course they want the relationship discouraged, just as much as Emma's mother does, saying he's no good for her –'

I shook my head. 'Really?' I said wryly. 'Whatever makes her think that?'

John nodded and closed the file. 'Quite, Casey. So that's where we're at. And it's a lot to think about so I do want you both to have a think.'

So no plunging in feet first, as I usually liked to do, then. And John was right to tell us to think because it was a great deal to take on. A newborn baby on its own would be a big physical challenge – babies were exhausting, full stop, for anyone. But to take on a newborn and a teen mum – one barely even into her teens in this case – would add a whole other layer of complication. She'd have her issues – how could she not, given her upbringing and current circumstances? – not to mention the ever-present spectre of having her baby taken away from her if she couldn't prove she was able to look after it. And what about this mum of hers? What might happen there? Much as I couldn't personally get my head round the idea of throwing out my

own daughter and grandson, I wasn't naïve either. This was
a woman with a long history of substance abuse and mental
illness, which meant all bets were off as far as good parent-
ing manuals were concerned. The poor girl. What a mess
to bring a new life into. She must be reeling and terrified,
the little mite.

I glanced at Mike, who was deep in thought as well. I
could tell. I met his eye, wondering if he was thinking what
I was – that we had to find a way to make this work.

'Look,' said John, 'don't rush into this. It's a huge under-
taking and I would absolutely understand if you didn't feel
it was for you. After all, most mother and baby carers go
through a specific course of training …'

'I've had two children,' I chipped in, 'both fully grown
now, not to mention two grandchildren, not to mention
eight foster kids and counting … it *is* eight, isn't it, Mike?'
I started pretending to count on my fingers.

John smiled at me. 'I'm *serious*, Casey. This is a complicated placement. With a great deal of potential for getting
even more complicated, as I'm sure you realise all too well.
Look, you know why I'm putting this to you. It's because I
think the two of you could handle it. Of course I do. But I
still have to talk it through with Emma's social worker
anyway. Plus the baby's – he'll obviously be allocated his
own social worker, if he hasn't been already. Which'll give
you two time to discuss it –' he pushed the buff folder
across the table to us. 'To read up properly, to consider the
implications and think it through before committing. A
new baby affects everything, as you both know all too well.

Means changing plans, not booking holidays, having your whole routine thrown into disarray …'

'Well,' said Mike, his positive tone of voice making my heart leap. 'It certainly does sound like something we should consider. But as you say,' he said, looking pointedly at me, 'we do need to weigh it up properly. Can you give us a day or so?'

John nodded as he rose from the table. 'Absolutely. As I say, I have to talk things through with the social workers anyway. And no doubt you'll want to have a chat with the rest of the clan, too.'

Which we would. The clan in question mainly being our daughter Riley and her partner David. If we were talking baby stuff, I doubted we'd be able to keep Riley away. She loved babies as much as I did, loved to immerse herself in children generally, and was also keen to help out whenever she could when we were fostering, because she and David had just finished the training to become foster carers themselves. We'd obviously also need to speak to our son Kieron. Though he no longer lived at home – he shared a flat with his long-term girlfriend Lauren – we never did anything that would impact on any member of the family without consulting them first. It wouldn't have been fair. Because John was right, having a new baby in the mix would change everything. Which would obviously affect everyone else.

But I was champing at the bit. And it must have been obvious because as soon as we'd waved John off Mike held his hand out. 'Come on,' he said, 'hand it over.'

He was talking about the file, which I'd picked up from the dining table as we'd shown John out.

'What?' I said, all innocent, seeing the firm set of his jaw line. I obediently gave him the file.

'You know very well what,' he answered, taking it. 'So how about you go and make more coffee while I dive in to this. I want a good read of what's in here before you dive on in at me. I have a feeling I'm going to need to be very clued up and alert before we have this next conversation.'

I laughed as I trotted off back into the kitchen. That husband of mine knows me so well.

Chapter 2

I yawned and stretched. It was one of those dark autumn mornings when the fact that you didn't need to get up and go anywhere made the duvet seem almost hypnotic. Just so soft and so cosy ... just fifteen minutes more, perhaps. I'd been having a particularly nice dream, after all. A bit bonkers, admittedly, but that was par for the course with me. My head was always so full of different people and their problems in the daytime, and then they all got scrambled up when my head hit the pillow and came back in different guises in my slumbers. This one was obviously related to the news John had brought to us, as it was chock full of babies: happy, smiley, sweet-smelling babies, which ... Yikes! The fifteen minutes had obviously turned into a whole hour. And then some. When I next checked the bedside clock it was nine forty-five!

There are days when it's okay to oversleep, and days when it isn't, and today was very much the latter, being the day we were going to have our second meeting about taking on Emma and her baby. I threw the covers off, knowing I'd better get my skates on and shower. Today was important, so both house and I had to look our best. I smiled to myself as I turned on the water; it was ironic that almost my last thought before falling asleep the previous evening was that I'd better make the most of any lie-ins I had left to me. With a three-week-old baby in the house they'd soon be in very short supply.

But I was getting ahead of myself. We hadn't actually agreed to that yet. Mike and I had discussed Emma at length on the Monday evening, after which he'd agreed I could call John and say yes only to taking the next step. 'No promises, though, Casey,' he'd warned, and I knew he'd meant it. 'We need to know exactly what's expected of us and we have to feel happy. Me in particular –' He'd fixed his eyes on me, to press the point home. 'I haven't forgotten the Sophia experience, not one bit.'

'Oh, don't be dramatic,' I rushed to answer, keen to keep him positive. 'We've had other foster kids since Sophia and they've been challenging as well, love …'

'Not teenage girls, Casey,' he shot back at me. 'With all their teenage girl behaviours. You might have forgotten all about that, but I certainly haven't.'

He was right to point it out, because of course I wanted to hurry past that. Sophia had been a teenage girl we'd fostered a few years back, and she had certainly been an eye opener. It had been only our second placement and I suppose we were still a bit inexperienced; certainly in regard to children as psychologically complex as she had been. She had been full-on, promiscuous, full of the usual teenage angst and lots more besides, and had come to us with only one mode of operation: flirt with the male of the species at all times. Not that it was her fault; she had become the way she had due to her terrible circumstances, and had learned flirting with men at her mother's knee, practically – as a good method of getting her way.

Until she came to us, that is, and in Mike found an immovable object that would remain so however hard she tried to be an unstoppable force. We came through it, thank goodness, and so were able to help her all the better for having been through so much with her. But when you're a middle-aged foster dad and have a fourteen-year-old foster daughter running around in her underwear, determined to create an impact, it's not a very nice place to be. It was equally distressing – if not more so – for our son Kieron, then just coming up to twenty-two, because she created some uncomfortable waves between him and his then brand-new girlfriend, Lauren.

We'd all learned to love Sophia, once we'd got past all that, but Mike had every right to make me sit down and think about things before plunging in with both feet again without thinking, like I usually did.

And I did think – we'd also run it by the children the previous evening, because their input was as important as our own. Riley, predictably, was as excited as I was. 'Oh, Mum, a baby? Oh, that will be such a lovely change for you.'

I grinned. 'Um, yes, it will,' I agreed, 'but not just a baby. This one does come with a teenaged mum attached, don't forget.'

'Yes, I know that, Mum,' she said. 'But you'll be fine. Teenagers to you are like toddlers are to me – easy peasy.'

I raised my eyebrows. Oh, really? I thought. She must have a short memory. Or just that selective amnesia that parents need to have, if every child in the world isn't to be an 'only'. Bless them, I loved them, but my grandsons had not been 'easy peasy' at all; they had been as demanding as any other little boys I ever knew, made worse by the fact that they were so close in age.

Still, I was flattered that Riley assumed teenagers were 'easy peasy' for me to handle, even if that wasn't strictly the case either. I did have some considerable experience of them to draw on, it had to be said, having spent many years handling them in large numbers in a behavioural unit in a high school, but dealing with kids in a school setting and having them in your home were two completely different things, as our experience of fostering so far had shown us.

But I was pleased Riley was happy for me, and felt so positive about it. It was generally Riley who sided with Mike in all situations where jumping in with both feet was my normal way of carrying on.

Kieron and Lauren had reacted in a similar fashion. They'd probably not be that involved in any case because they were both busy with their own lives. Right now, specifically, they revolved around working as many hours as they could manage, to save up for getting their own place.

'It's up to you and Dad,' Kieron had said, laughing, when I asked him how he felt about it. 'I don't even know why you feel you have to ask us, because you'll only do what you want to do anyway!'

I jumped out of the shower, towelled myself dry and began to ferret in my wardrobe for something suitable to wear. Kieron was right, I supposed, though I'd keep asking him anyway. Because one day he might have strong opinions about a placement, and I knew that however headstrong I was I would respect that. In the short term, however, I had to get a move-on. Mike was taking time off from work to attend this afternoon's meeting, so would be home before I knew it, for an early lunch.

And then we'd be up and running – and there was no mistaking the little shiver of excitement I felt about it. And also intrigue. The start of a new placement didn't just mean getting to know a new child – in this case, children – but also the start of a new relationship with the child's social worker, too, and I wondered what this one might be like. It might be someone I'd worked with already, of course; I'd certainly had dealings with plenty over the years. But in reality that had never actually happened. Every new child seemed to come with a new social worker, too, so it was no surprise that I didn't recognise the name of this one.

Her name was Maggie Cunliffe, and I wondered what she was like. With the name Maggie, I pictured her to be in her mid-forties to fifties, which pleased me for some reason. I tutted to myself – how very ageist of me!

The truth was, of course, that good social workers, like the kids in their charge, came in all sorts of shapes and sizes. I'd met young, fresh-faced types, just out of university and keen as mustard, right through to the battle-worn, tattered-suited, ready-for-retirement types. Where would Maggie fit in here, I wondered? Well, we would soon see.

Very soon, as it turned out, the already short morning having disappeared from beneath me, with Mike dashing in with less than fifteen minutes to spare. And my response to his greeting of 'Get the kettle on, love, will you? While I run up and shower' was greeted, in return, by my usual pre-meeting answer of 'Don't you dare leave so much as a drip on my bathroom floor!'

I was always a bit like this when an important meeting loomed. I'd done the house from top to bottom yesterday but I still felt I could do more. I'm a bit of a clean-freak and was characteristically anxious in case I'd missed some speck of dust or splash of water somewhere. Ridiculous, really, since neither John nor Maggie would be up inspecting my bathroom, but even so I just couldn't help it.

'Now, remember,' Mike warned me, having come back down and joined me at the dining table, 'we're here to listen to what they have to say; to mull it all over and consider the possibilities. Not to immediately ask when the girl can move in, okay?'

'Oh, be quiet, Mike,' I chided him. 'I'm not a child, you know. Anyway, they're here now,' I added, gesturing to the car that was pulling up outside. 'Go on,' I said. 'Go let them in.'

I smoothed my blouse down over my jeans and glanced again out of the window as Mike did so, childishly pleased to see that I'd been right; Maggie Cunliffe looked exactly like a Maggie. Mid-forties or thereabouts, I decided, with a lovely warm expression and curly blonde hair. She was also, I noticed appreciatively, dressed in jeans and a warm jumper. Nothing prim or proper about her. I felt immediately at ease.

The file itself, however, looked rather more daunting. Introductions done, the coffee poured, the biscuits politely declined – so far – it appeared out of Maggie's briefcase and landed on the table with a dull thud. Which was unusual. It was normally the case that we had almost nothing to go on, and had to find out the extent of a child's difficulties the hard way.

Not so here, clearly. Maggie dived straight in with a summary.

'Emma's mum was only sixteen when she had Emma,' she began. She had a soft Scottish accent, which seemed to go just perfectly with her name. 'There was no boyfriend – again, there's no knowledge of who the father was – and, as you already know, Shelley – that's her name – has battled with her demons since we've known her. She's an only child herself and has long since been estranged from her own mother, and has a long history of substance abuse. Various addictions have been on file here: alcohol, prescription medicines, as well as an array of illegal drugs. During her worst periods – and there have been quite a few down the years – she's had Emma placed into care, or had the authorities just step in and take her, but, because she never objected and so often put Emma in care voluntarily, a court order's never been sought.

'Every now and then,' Maggie continued, 'Shelley would sign herself up for rehab, get clean, and then come out determined to step up to the plate and take proper care of her daughter, but of course the harsh reality is that with each new episode of this kind she was just chipping away at Emma's trust.' Maggie sighed. 'So, as night follows day, each time Emma went back into care – and the older she got – the more and more she felt she didn't need her mum. It's a really sad one, this.' She glanced up and looked directly at me. 'You can see how the picture's formed here, can't you, Casey? And it's why we've ended up with the Emma we have today.'

I nodded sadly. I could see it all too clearly. She'd be feeling lost, hurting lots and desperately needing some attachment. In my years working with teenagers I'd seen so many like her; girls who'd gone on to get pregnant at such a tragically early age simply to stop an ache that they had inside them. It was partly a need to nurture, a need to have at least something – someone – to call their own, to replace the pain of not having a mother's love and affection.

'I can indeed,' I agreed, visualising this poor child so very well. 'And we're up to speed with the situation with the boyfriend, as well. John's filled us in there.'

'Yes, indeed,' John confirmed. 'So the next stage, if you wouldn't mind, Maggie, is to fill Casey and Mike in – well, fill all of us in, actually – about anything extra that has to happen, given this is a mother and baby placement. I'm not fully conversant; is there some extra training that might need to be involved?'

Maggie shook her head. 'Not in this case, I don't think. If you were new to fostering, obviously, or if you'd not brought up your own kids, but, no, in this case, I wouldn't insult your intelligence. It's obviously not going to be like your usual programme – no points system for Emma to follow or anything – just gentle guidance; it's more a case of both providing a loving, supportive, non-judgemental home for the two of them, and helping Emma take responsibility for taking care of her child herself.'

I nodded. There was a world of difference between that and being looked after. Emma was Roman's mother and had to be a mother to him. It would be all too easy for her to slip into a completely different, more dependent role, were she allowed to. I'd seen it happen myself. And it was understandable to some extent, as any mother would probably know; even if your child becomes a mother they are still very much your child, so if they were thirteen or fourteen – even fifteen and sixteen – the urge to mother both child and grandchild would be strong. I would have to guard against doing that, for definite, because it was the sort of thing that would feel so natural to do.

Mike must have been reading my thoughts.

'How much "help" would this entail, specifically?' he asked Maggie. 'I mean, you obviously wouldn't want us taking over, here. She'd have to do all the usual baby-related tasks herself?'

Maggie lifted a hand and waggled it slightly in front of her as if to indicate there was a degree of give and take here, that we'd have to use our judgement about how strict the division of labour needed to be in this specific situation. 'Well, in normal circumstances – whatever "normal" is – yes, that's what we'd expect. However, in this case, we do have to make some allowances. Emma obviously hasn't had the usual sort of upbringing. No younger or older siblings, no extended family, no experience of babies. The place she's at now is that she seems to be coping quite well; with the support of the baby's social worker, who stops by a few times a week to teach her the basics, she is coming on okay. Roman's social worker also has to record supervisory visits, where she's been noting down Emma's ability to care. She'll continue to do this, obviously, because it really is central to the placement. It's on the basis of those visits that the court will eventually decide if Emma's fit to look after her child on her own.'

There was a short silence after Maggie said this, as perhaps there would be. This wasn't just a case of us providing a home for a young mother. Our home would be the stage on which both mother and baby's whole future would be played out. At some point – and it only just hit me at that moment – someone other than me *would* stand in judgement over Emma and make a decision that would affect their whole lives.

'Wow,' I said quietly, as it sank in how much this period mattered. How much my input or otherwise might affect things. 'Does this happen with all underage mums or just those in care?'

'In theory, all of them,' Maggie explained. 'When a young girl like Emma becomes pregnant, it doesn't matter what her background is. The midwives are obliged to inform social services. They also have to record how responsible the teen is; whether she attends appointments, takes advice, eats healthily, plans properly for when the child is born … And, because of this, social services are alerted where it appears help may be required – and that's whether the child's in care or otherwise.'

I nodded my understanding. 'So,' John said, picking up his pen, 'do we know who the baby's social worker is?'

Maggie rustled through her paperwork. 'Hannah Greenwood. She's visiting three times a week at present, but if Casey and Mike take Emma on we'd probably cut that down to two, then after a while, if things are going okay, one.'

'And how long is all this for?' Mike asked.

Maggie shrugged. 'How long is a piece of string?' Then she grimaced. 'Sorry – that's not very helpful of me, is it? But, in truth, it's impossible to say. In some cases it's evident in a matter of a few weeks that the mother's capable and has a strong attachment to her baby, whereas in others – well, sometimes, it takes longer to tell.'

I looked at Mike. It was really sinking in now that this was a lot to take on. We weren't just providing a place of safety, a warm and loving home. We would be part of the process. There was also the small matter – no, the *huge* matter – of our own attachments. It wouldn't just be Emma who'd be forming a bond with her baby. We would be too. We'd be fools to think otherwise.

And I knew how I was around babies. It would be impossible for me to see this as just a job, and Mike knew that. But at the same time I knew that I wanted to accept this placement, even knowing that the end of it would probably break my heart. 'What happens at the end?' I asked Maggie.

She glanced at John before answering. 'It depends on the outcome, Casey. If all goes well, Emma and Roman will move on to a sort of halfway house; in a unit with maybe one or two other young mums and their babies until she's legally old enough to live on her own. We'd assist her then, obviously, with getting a place to live. But if things don't go to plan, then we'll have to think again, obviously. But let's not dwell on the bleak side just yet, eh? Hopefully we'll get a happy ending out of this.'

Happy endings. You didn't hear of them so often in this game. Sometimes, yes, and we'd had our share of them, even if 'happy' was always qualified – those damaged pasts couldn't just be spirited away that easily. But if we could have a happy ending for this child-mum and her baby, that would be fantastic.

I was still musing on just how fantastic it would be when Mike did something entirely out of character. Coughing slightly, to get my attention, he looked pointedly at me. 'I think we're of a mind about this,' he said. 'Aren't we, Casey?' He then looked at John and Maggie. 'We'd like to give it a shot,' he said, before I'd even opened my mouth to answer. 'That is, if you two think we're up for it.'

Well, I thought, having to haul my jaw back into position. Now, that was a turn-up for the books.

Chapter 3

In the normal course of events before taking on a new foster child, the next few days (following Mike's jaw-dropping but very pleasing agreement to us having Emma) would involve a meeting between the three of us – us and the child, so that we could see if we all felt we clicked. This was obviously sensible; for all the discussions over coffee and plates of biscuits, meeting the child who was potentially going to share your home and lives for several months was an essential part of the process. Suppose she hated us on sight? Suppose we felt we wouldn't be able to bond with her? It hadn't happened yet – well, not from Mike and my point of view, anyway – but that certainly didn't mean it couldn't. And better to say no than to get a placement under way and then terminate it. For a younger child, in particular, this could be extremely emotionally challenging. The children we fostered had already known so much rejection that to inflict more, by getting their hopes up and then deciding we didn't want to have them, would be noth-ing short of cruel.

But in this case we were happy to go with Maggie's instinct.

'She's so excited,' she said. 'I've told her all about you and the family, and she really can't wait to move in.'

I took this with a slight pinch of salt. I didn't doubt Emma would be happy to get settled somewhere – anywhere – but I didn't imagine for a moment that 'excited' would be her principal emotion. I also wondered if there was pressure being brought to bear on the situation by the mum of the girl she was currently staying with. If so, better she come straight to us than have the upheaval (a new baby is upheaval enough anyway) of having to move somewhere else as a temporary measure.

And, well, a bit of me was pleased to hear she was pleased. We'd be fine together. I didn't doubt it for a moment.

Over the past few days my house had been a hive of activity, and I had taken no prisoners. It was all hands on deck and, boy, did the family know it. No stone would be left unturned in my quest to seek out dust and destroy.

'Honestly, Mum,' Riley had said to me, exasperated, when I dispatched her into town to get a new duvet set, 'the house is already perfect as it is! You have the beige bedroom all ready and you have the blue bedroom all ready. Which covers both bases. If she has the cot in with her – which she probably will – they can both go in the beige room and, if not, Roman can go in the blue room. Why on earth,' she asked pointedly, 'do you need new bedding?'

She was right, of course. She generally was in such matters. It was just my natural urge to do something extra to make them welcome. And it was an urge that had back-fired with the last kids we'd fostered. It had seemed such a great idea to decorate one room pink and one room blue (all fostering eventualities catered for – ta-da!) till John Fulshaw gave us two unrelated nine-year-old boys, who could no more have shared a room when they arrived than fly.

Which was also why the pink room was now, in fact, the beige room, because it just so happened that the second boy, Georgie, was autistic, and as soon as he saw the pink room he freaked out (to use the professional term) because pink really, really upset him. So the moral of the story is don't assume *anything*. Don't prejudge what a child might or might not like.

But I never learn, and Riley knew that, and she duly went off to find a cheap and cheerful duvet set, as instructed, if only in the cause of calming me down.

Today, though, I was all of a flap again, as usual going through my lists – I'm at the age when I can't function without my lists – for the umpteenth time. Riley had come over again, having dropped Levi at school and Jackson at nursery, just to help me finish off and to say hello. As a young mum herself, I knew Riley's presence would be a positive one for Emma; one that wouldn't smack so much of being faced with a posse of know-all middle-aged women, but more of introducing a like-minded friend.

'Right,' she said, as the time for them to arrive grew ever nearer. 'Put that list away, and that's an order, Mum. You've gone through it countless times already and you have everything you need.'

'But what if she hasn't got any baby milk or something?'

Riley shook her head. 'Mum, you don't live in Antarctica, you know. If she needs milk, then you can pop out and get some. Anyway, you don't know what type she uses so it would have been pointless to stock up anyway. And, trust me; she will have enough milk. That also applies to the steriliser, the baby bath, the cot mobile, the muslins and all the other silly things on your list.'

'It's a very sensible list,' I huffed as I walked to the window to look out for them. 'Oh shit!' I added, seeing a car pull up. 'They're here!'

I had a room spray in my hand, so I chucked it now at Riley. 'Have a quick spray around with that, will you, while I let them in?'

She didn't grace my order with a reply. Instead she just calmly put the aerosol in the dining-room cupboard. 'Mum, you know something?' she said finally. 'You are just a teensy bit cuckoo. Go on, let them in. I'll go and pop the kettle on.'

I took a deep breath, as I always did, before opening the front door, ready to see what sort of child might be on the other side. My first impression – my gut instinct – was something I had learned to trust over the years. You could tell so much about a child from that first sweep of information gathering; from the basics of what their clothes and accent said about the sort of world they'd come from, to the less obvious pointers, such as how they responded to you, and what that said about their personality and confidence. Were they frightened? Full of attitude? Traumatised? It wasn't quite Sherlock Holmes territory, but it was an inner voice that had rarely been wrong.

'Well, hello!' I said, beaming at the little congregation on the doorstep.

I didn't immediately take stock of Emma, however, because my eye was drawn to the car seat that was hanging from Maggie's elbow, and the well-wrapped and fast-asleep bundle it contained. I dragged my gaze away, however, to greet the person I knew must be my main focus – his mother.

'You must be Emma,' I said, taking in how slight she was, how young-looking, how not at all her fourteen years. She was tiny, with blonde hair tied back into a side ponytail and enormous blue eyes. Ironic, but she looked the picture of chaste innocence. 'Oh,' I gushed, 'and your baby is just gorgeous. Come on. Come on in. Follow me.'

Now, I've met some reluctant-looking kids in my time, obviously, but it had been a long time since I'd seen an expression quite as defiant and disdainful as the one etched on this particular teenager's face. As I ushered the three of them in, I made my smile all the wider to compensate. Hmm, I thought. Whatever happened to the 'oh, she's so excited' line from Maggie?

Still, this was probably par for the course, I decided, as I showed them into the dining area. It was the kind of attitude that was commonly seen in lots of teenagers, that whole scowly, cocky attitude thing she had going on. Standard teenager-ese, as portrayed in many a TV programme, and which reminded me that being a mother doesn't stop a girl being a typical fourteen-year-old; it might eventually, and probably would, by sheer force of circumstance, but right now this was a teenager who just happened to have had a baby. Which didn't stop her looking and acting like a teenager.

Riley, who was finishing off preparing refreshments, stood in the kitchen archway and beamed too. 'Hi everyone!' she said. 'Drinks orders, please!'

I was pleased to note a slight but perceptible softening of Emma's features on seeing my daughter. She'd obviously been told about Riley and now I could see her wondering how this young, cool and clearly more on-her-wavelength kind of person might fit into her life while she was with us.

'That's my daughter,' I said to her as we all sat down at the table. 'She doesn't live here but she visits all the time. She has boys too – two of them. Levi and Jackson. I expect Maggie's told you about them, hasn't she? You'll get to meet them in the next few days.'

This seemed to spark a return to the previous scowl. 'If I'm here in a few days,' she was quick to point out. 'I told her,' she said, glancing across at Maggie pointedly, 'that I'm going to have to see how it goes first.'

Okaaayyy, I thought. I'm getting the real picture now, which is fine. I was just about to answer – with something agreeing that that was a perfectly reasonable point – when Maggie, looking apologetic, spoke first. 'Sorry, Casey,' she said, looking equally pointedly at her young charge. 'But Emma's having something of a stroppy day today, aren't you? Didn't much like getting up at six to get here, did you?'

Had I paid more attention to that I might have had more of a clue about the shape of things to come, but of course I didn't. I just brushed over it and tried to jolly things along. 'Six in the morning?' I exclaimed. 'That would be enough to give anyone a bad case of the grumps. But at least you're here now, and I'm sure you'll get a chance to catch up on a bit of sleep later.'

And I did feel for her. A new baby was exhausting. And though I'd forgotten quite how exhausted I'd been with my own two newborns, I'd certainly been reminded when Riley had had hers. That old 'sleep when the baby sleeps' mantra was all very well in theory. But in practice there always seemed to be a million things that needed doing in those precious few pockets of time.

Riley brought the drinks in then and said her goodbyes for the moment, and as she left it occurred to me that Roman, in his car seat, was still on the floor at Maggie's side, rather than with Emma. I also realised, as Maggie started chatting about the placement, that Emma didn't as much as glance in his direction. Which perhaps should have rung alarm bells as well but didn't, not really – she was so young and so shell shocked, after all.

And that state of affairs continued all through Maggie's initial briefing; while she explained that Hannah – Roman's social worker – would be joining us shortly, just giving us time to get the handover documents sorted. This was usual. There were all sorts of different forms that needed going through, including risk assessments, medical consent forms and so on.

'Tell you what,' Maggie said to Emma as she began sorting bits of paper. 'While we get on with the boring stuff why don't you get Roman's hat and coat and things off? He'll be due a feed by the time Hannah gets here, won't he?'

As if to prompt Emma, she pushed the car seat over to where Emma was sitting and I watched as Emma pulled it close enough to start unbuckling the seat straps. She turned to look at me. 'Hannah's just a nosy cow,' she said to me, entirely without prompting. 'She just wants to catch me out doing something wrong.' I was slightly shocked; it seemed quite a forward thing for her to say. And she wasn't finished. 'Make sure you take notes, by the way. Because that's what you're supposed to be doing as well.'

I didn't rise to it. Instead I put my pen down and smiled at her. 'I'm sure Hannah's just doing her job, Emma,' I said levelly. 'But I can assure you – cross my heart – that I'm not here to try and catch you out. I'm sure you're going to do just great, I really am. And I'm here to help. Help when you ask me to, okay?'

Emma snorted then. 'Yeah, right!' she said, her voice full of venom. 'That's exactly what Hannah said to me when she first came. Trust me, lady,' she went on, 'she's just look-ing for the first excuse she finds to take my kid!'

I was saddened, rather than shocked, by the tone of Emma's voice. Just a few weeks into motherhood, which was destabilising enough already, and she was living in such an uncertain world. And a scary one, too. For all that it was not the desired outcome, there was a kernel of truth there – if she 'failed', social services would indeed take her kid. And she was just a little girl herself. A frightened little girl with no one to turn to. And fear can make anyone lash out.

By now Emma had unbuckled the seat and pulled the baby onto her lap, and right away I felt my own fears subside a little. In contrast to her demeanour earlier, now she actually had her baby in her arms she had eyes for no one but him. She also seemed confident, if understandably careful, supporting his head the way she needed to and gently rocking him back and forth. It was only when Hannah herself arrived that her expression was once again stony. 'Oh, look, Roman,' she said, as I showed his social worker into the dining area, 'it's the kiddie collector, come to check I haven't poisoned your bottle.'

Now I was slightly shocked, because she'd said this to Hannah's face. But Hannah just smiled. Like Emma, she was blonde, with her hair corralled into a neat ponytail, and perhaps in her late twenties, I guessed. She had the no-nonsense air of a capable big sister, and I was sad that so far she and Emma obviously hadn't bonded. Not that they didn't have a bit of repartee going on. Or a semblance of it, at least – though maybe it wasn't that. Perhaps it was all one-way traffic on Hannah's part to try and jolly Emma on. I hoped their lack of closeness wouldn't affect how things played out.

'Ah, I see you're on form today, Emma,' she said mildly. 'That's good. I think I'd start to worry if you actually let up a bit!' She began unbuttoning her coat, a fur-trimmed khaki parka. 'I would properly introduce myself,' she said to me, 'but I see my reputation precedes me!'

It was an interesting dynamic and I was anxious to take it in. So while Hannah began outlining her role and how she and Maggie would work together, I kept an eye on Emma too, and what she was doing. And what she was doing was calmly getting on with the business of feeding Roman, holding him snugly in her left arm while reaching into her bag to retrieve his bottle.

'Do you have a microwave?' she asked me politely, when there was a lull in the conversation.

'Yes, of course,' I said, pointing out where to find it in the kitchen. I then watched as she stood up and, with Roman still in her arms, went and used it, returning and sitting down again with baby and bottle and giving him his feed.

'Right,' she said amiably, as the tiny child began sucking lustily on the warmed milk. 'Where were we? Oh, yes, the kiddie collector was about to tell you how best to spy on me, was that it?' She met Hannah's eye then. 'Carry on.'

All very curious. And should alarm bells have been ringing? I had absolutely no idea.

Chapter 4

Emma's possessions – which had been lugged in by her and Roman's long-suffering social workers – came in four bulging and already torn black bin liners. This was nothing new to me; in my time I'd seen it all. Some kids came with almost nothing and some with loads of possessions, and it was often the ones who'd been the longest in care who had the most stuff to lug about. Similarly, some children had a variety of robust cases, while others – as in this case – just had good old bin bags. But in those cases you expected to find them filled with rags and rubbish – and invariably you weren't disappointed.

It was always a bit of a guessing game when new children came to stay as to what their possessions might be. Some had plenty of clothes, shoes and trainers, favourite toys, games and books, right down to nightwear and their own toiletries and toothbrush. Others had barely more than the clothes they stood up in. No toys, no nice things, not even a single family photo, and when that happened it really broke my heart. I just wanted to scoop them up and promise them the world, though, ironically, that was usually the last thing I could do. These tended to be the kids that had been profoundly damaged by the adults around them, and the sad fact was that the children who needed the most loving always seemed to be the ones who needed you to keep your distance – in the early days, at least, until they'd begun the lengthy process of learning to trust again.

Emma and Roman, thankfully, didn't seem to be in this category. Although, judging from my first impressions, Emma had plenty of emotional issues to overcome, she wasn't in need when it came to material possessions. 'Good grief!' I said, once we'd seen off Maggie and Hannah. 'What on earth have you got in all these?'

She laughed as we hefted a pair each up the stairs, which was good to hear. Now we were alone – and unscrutinised – she seemed in better spirits. 'Oh, just my clothes and make-up, and my CD player, and Roman's stuff and every-thing. Tell you what,' she said conversationally, 'social services may be arseholes, but they've spent loads on me. Literally. Like, loads.'

That was true enough. We'd already taken delivery of a pristine new cot, which Mike had toiled to assemble the night before Emma came. But I was struck by her choice of language for them – and not in a good way. I was about to answer, not least to pull her up on her choice of words, when she turned, having reached the top of the stairs. 'And they're going to buy me a laptop – can you believe it? Long as I go back to school, that is. Can you *believe* that?'

I could believe that, of course, because, these days, a computer was fast becoming more than an optional extra; kids were expected to produce their school assignments at a keyboard more and more, not to mention use the internet for research. Which meant disadvantaged kids – and Emma was very much in that category – were at more of a disadvantage than they'd been in many, many years, compared with kids from affluent middle-class homes.

Emma pouted then. 'But that's not going to be for ages, is it? I wish they'd let me have one now. I hate being so much out of touch with everyone.'

I understood that too. So much teenage communication was via computers that I could see how isolated not having one must make her feel. Not that I wasn't all for policing the use of them, particularly for the kids we looked after, because you could access so much stuff that no kid should ever see.

'I know,' I said, gesturing that she should go into the beige bedroom, which was all set now, with its cheerful new coordinating duvet set. 'But it'll be sooner than you think – and you really should go back to school. And, in the meantime, I have a laptop that I'm happy to let you borrow – you just have to ask me. Just one thing …'

I paused then and, noticing the sudden silence, Emma turned. 'The language,' I said mildly. 'Now you're with us you're going to have to mind your tongue a bit. I don't know what experiences you've had with Hannah and

Maggie, obviously, but, well, social services are lots of things, but not what you called them.'

Emma looked at me, assessing me, and with a look of slight confusion. I grinned at her. 'Oh, don't worry,' I said. 'I'm not shocked. I'm used to teenagers – I've brought up two of my own, don't forget. And we'll treat you just as if you were one of our own, as well, which means that even if you swear when you're out and about we don't want to hear it at home, okay?'

Emma was the one looking shocked now. 'But I didn't swear, did I?'

I nodded. 'Sweetheart,' I said mildly, 'you called social services "arseholes", which in my book is swearing. And, colourful as it may be, it's not something I like to hear from a young lady. I'm not a prude but I just don't think it sounds very nice – particularly coming from a young mum.'

I was surprised and pleased to see that she had the grace to look ashamed. 'I'm sorry,' she said quietly. 'I didn't even realise. I'm just that used to it. I'll try not to do it again, promise.'

I was touched. After all her aggressive bluster earlier, this was quite a contrast, and once again I was struck by her child-like vulnerability. And not even child-like – she *was* a child, one that had been thrust into the world of adults. And yet without any adult family to take care of her. I often wondered how it was that the kids we took in so often seemed to have absolutely no one to love them. And equally often I reminded myself that it was precisely the reason why they came to us. Because there was no one else willing

37

to take them in. No indulgent auntie, no older sibling, no grandparents, no nothing. Emma was an only daughter, born to an only daughter – one who'd fallen out with her mother before Emma had even been born. It was all so very sad. And now there was Roman, equally lacking a wider family … I mentally shook myself. Mustn't go there, Casey.

I pulled open the wardrobe doors while Emma began busying herself taking CDs from one of the bags. These kids and their CDs – music was pretty much all digital now, as far as I was aware, but these kids seemed to pride themselves on being 'old school', in the same way as we'd hung on to our 'authentic' LPs, distrusting the dawning of the digital disc.

Bless her, I thought, as she began stacking them up. 'I know you will, love,' I reassured her. 'So as far as I'm concerned, the subject is now closed. And look – enough space in here for everything, I think. Do you want me to help you put things away?'

She nodded at me shyly. 'Yes, please.'

'Great,' I said, seeing the CD player which was now in her hand. 'And perhaps listen to music! Seeing as Roman's fast asleep downstairs, how about we have some on while we unpack, eh?' I reached for one of the CDs she'd begun to stack on the chest of drawers. 'This looks good. Hey, we can dance while we work!'

In common with many a teenager before her, Emma looked horrified at this thought. She looked at me, then at the CD, and then back at me again. It was the sort of look I knew well. It said 'Whaaattt?'

'Only kidding,' I reassured her, passing her the rap CD and laughing. 'My days of dancing to this sort of thing are long over. If indeed, I ever had them, truth be known. But put it on anyway, eh? Or something else you like. I don't mind which. Just be nice to help you start to feel at home.'

But as I spoke, and Emma duly took the proffered CD from my hand, I noticed this small but distinct furrowing of her child's smooth, unworried brow. And as I was something of an expert in the non-verbal communication habits of teenagers, I could tell right away what it meant, too. It meant 'Home? You stupid woman. What's "home"?'

'So, what do you think?' I said to Mike, once I'd come back downstairs. I'd made a start helping Emma put her bits and bobs away, as promised, but then left her to it, telling her I'd check on Roman for her. I was conscious that perhaps she'd like a little space.

My big hulk of a macho husband, who'd come home from work early, just before Maggie and Hannah had left, was peering into the pram with a big soppy grin on his face.

'About this one?' he whispered, glancing up at me. He stepped away, but kept his voice low as he spoke. 'He seems like a good 'n. Not been a peep out of him since you've been up there.' He motioned towards the ceiling with his eyebrows. 'And how about his mum?'

He'd spoken to Emma only briefly so far, having only had the chance to say hello to her really, straight after Maggie and Hannah had left.

'So far, so pretty much what I'd have expected,' I told him. 'Fair bit of attitude, particularly towards Hannah – you know, the blonde one you met? She's Roman's social worker. But then I suppose that's understandable, given what her role is.' I looked into the pram too. 'And by all accounts she's been lucky. So far, at any rate. It would have been so much more difficult if he hadn't been such a placid little thing – which he has, by all accounts, so Hannah tells me.'

I looked again at the little bundle of life nestled beneath the covers, and, as if on cue, he opened his enormous eyes and seemed to consider me. He really was the most beautiful little boy. His eyes were so dark that they seemed almost black, and his skin was a lovely olive colour. His head was sprigged, more than covered, in little chocolate-brown tufts, and thinking about Emma and her pale colouring I wondered about his father and what he might look like. I said as much to Mike, too, in what I hoped sounded like a casual sort of manner, though, in truth, it was anything but.

Seeing this tiny infant and wondering what the future might hold for him, I couldn't help thinking back to Justin, the first boy we'd fostered, and how never knowing who his father was had eaten away at him. And even though, when he did find the man, the outcome wasn't quite a happy ever after, just knowing he was there had gone such a way to heal that wound. I remembered his exact words to me. He said he just felt 'more whole'.

Mike frowned and shook his head. 'Typical you,' he said. 'Casey,' he then warned, 'don't even go there, love. I thought we agreed we wouldn't go down that road – not unless we have to, at any rate.'

'I'm just saying,' I said, tutting. 'Just wondering, that's all.'

But Mike was having none of it. He straightened up and made for the door. 'I know what you're like, love, once you get to "just wondering". And you know as well as I do where it can lead.'

I knew exactly what he was talking about. I knew exactly who he was talking about – a girl we'd looked after the previous year, Abby. Abby's mum had MS and told everyone she was all alone in the world – not a single relative to call on – but I knew there was more to it than that. There was actually a sister; an auntie who was desperate to support both of them, but with whom Abby's mum had fallen out. Of course, I couldn't help but poke my nose in, and I'd paid the price for it. It had resulted in an official complaint against me and a really stressful investigation; an experience I would not want to repeat. But him mentioning that was like a red rag to a bull.

'Mike,' I chided, 'that's so unfair. It was my "wondering" and all my digging that reunited their flipping family!'

Which was true. And I'd been exonerated, and Abby's mum had apologised to me, profusely. But it might have worked out differently, as we both knew.

'Yes, but it also might have reunited you with your last P45 too, love,' Mike reminded me. 'And, don't forget, this ex-boyfriend sounds like he's a wrong 'un. Perhaps that little man there is better off without him in his life. Anyway, I'm off to put the kettle on. Coffee?'

I nodded, and turned my attention back to the baby. I had just been wondering. I wasn't about to go sleuthing. I had no intention of lifting the lid on that potential can of worms. Emma was right to be reluctant to name the baby's father; after all, technically, he'd committed an offence just by *being* the baby's father, given Emma's age. Mike was right. Best not to even go there.

'So we won't,' I whispered to Roman who was now properly stirring, stretching his little limbs and blinking, fixing his gaze once again on me. I smiled at him – how could anyone not automatically smile at a baby? – and reached into the pram to pick him up. He gurgled as I nestled him gently against my shoulder and breathed in his distinctive baby scent. I loved sniffing babies; they always smelt so good, even if this one, at this particular time, had another smell going on – one that wasn't quite so attractive as baby talc.

I wrinkled my nose as I carried him to the foot of the stairs, thinking I'd call Emma downstairs to change him. But as soon as I got there I could hear the thump of the music overhead and realised there was little chance she'd hear me.

'No worries, little man,' I whispered into the baby's ear. 'Auntie Casey will change your bottom for you, eh?'

I took Roman back into the living room and grabbed a blanket from the pram to lie him down on. So much for Riley's dismissive 'you won't need to buy baby stuff' – there'd been no sign of a changing mat amongst Emma's things that I'd seen. Still, I thought, as I lay him down, we could soon see to that. The thought made me smile. I was quite looking forward to going baby shopping again.

I was just reaching for the bag that was hanging on the pram handle when Mike returned, brandishing two coffees.

'Casey,' he asked pointedly, 'should it be you who's doing that?'

I waved a dismissive hand. 'Oh, it's fine, love. Just for today, at any rate. Emma's still busy putting her thousand and one possessions away upstairs, and she's got to get the bedding on the cot too, don't forget. Better I do it this once than have her break off when she's busy moving in properly. Don't worry – I won't be making a habit of butting in. I'll make sure she does it from tomorrow on.'

Mike put my coffee down on the table behind me. 'I wasn't just thinking of that, love. I was thinking of Emma. Don't you think she might have issues with someone else doing these things for her? You know what my sister was like – wouldn't so much as let anyone breathe near little Natalie. How d'you know Emma won't feel the –'

He stopped then, and I turned to see why. Emma's ears must have been burning, because she was now standing in the living-room doorway.

'Hello, love,' Mike began. 'Did you find everything you needed upstairs okay?'

'I hope you don't mind, sweetheart,' I added, as I quickly finished changing and re-dressing Roman. 'Only he needed changing and I thought it best to let you get on.'

I made to hold him out to her, but she glanced at Mike and then back at me, making no move to take him. Instead she nodded. 'It's fine,' she said. 'I only came down to get a glass of water. If you want to play with him for a bit more, I don't mind. I can finish our room off then, can't I? You know, if you like.'

'Oh, of course,' I said, snuggling the baby back against my shoulder automatically. 'He's such a good little boy; no trouble at all. You get yourself a drink and get finished. Mike and I will mind him.'

'Thanks,' Emma said, disappearing into the kitchen to get her water. 'Oh, and by the way,' she called back through, 'have you got one of those adaptor thingies?'

'Adaptors?' Mike asked. 'What kind of adaptor?'

Emma came back in, holding a glass of water. 'You know,' she said. 'So you can plug a few things in one socket at the same time. Only I need to charge my phone because I'm, um, expecting a call later, and there's already the bedside lamp plugged in there. Well, the CD player right now, obviously, but I just wondered for, like, later. Unless there's another plug somewhere? I didn't see one.'

'There's another socket behind the bed,' I said. 'You can plug the bedside lamp in there if you like. I'm sure it'll reach.'

'Sweet,' she said. 'Great. Okay.' She glanced at Roman. 'Okay, I'll be down in a bit then.'

I knew what was coming as soon as Emma had gone back upstairs. I'd answered automatically, but not without it flipping a mental switch with me. There were protocols for dealing with such things. As Mike well knew too.

'A phone?' he said, frowning. 'In her bedroom and unsupervised? And a call from who exactly? She seemed cagey about that, didn't you think?' He sighed. 'I can see this becoming complicated, can't you?'

I knew what he meant, but didn't share his anxiety. She hadn't seemed cagey to me. If she'd wanted to be cagey she would have just plugged her phone in anyway, and made do with not having a bedside light, surely? Teenagers were notoriously obsessive about their privacy, but there was nothing in Emma's tone that made me anxious about letting her have her phone, even if we did need to be clear on what the protocol was.

And there was always a protocol. There were protocols for everything in our line of work. Mike was right – with a young teenager like this we'd normally prohibit the use of a mobile up in their bedroom – and for obvious reasons. The children we looked after weren't in any way the average; they often had dark and difficult pasts, and all the dark and difficult associations that kind of background tended to throw up. In some cases there might be family members wanting to snatch them back, even, which was why communication with families had to be supervised and managed, and our home address guarded as if it were a state secret. The risk to us, from some of the families whose children we took in, was very real and could not be underestimated. Though this was different. Well, as far as we knew, anyway. Emma's mum had always put her in care voluntarily. And she was only with us now because of the baby. This wasn't one of our 'last chance saloon' troubled kids, where violence and criminality were family norms.

'Leave it with me, love,' I said to Mike. 'I'll check with Maggie tomorrow morning. I know we wouldn't normally allow it, but perhaps it's not the issue it normally is in this case. Plus she might feel more secure having her phone close to her.'

Mike wasn't convinced, though. 'Or to conduct a whole life that we're not privy to, more likely. You know what teenagers are like, love – always good at giving you the edited highlights of what they're up to.'

Yes I did, and I'd known a fair few of them too. But that had been in my last job – not when it came to the ones we fostered. And that was precisely because mobile phone use was controlled. I still thought he was being just a little over-cautious, and we also mustn't forget that Emma was a young mum – she had adult responsibilities now so we should at least grant her a few adult benefits. But I'd call Maggie anyway, just to put his mind at rest. Even if I knew he was worrying about nothing.

But it turned out that Mike was perhaps a little more perceptive than I was. It was in the small hours, around two, when I woke up that night. Woke up with a start, moreover, confused by what I was hearing. Was that a baby crying? Disorientated by the sound, I thought I was imagining it for a moment, and then my brain caught up – of course it was. We had a baby in the house now, didn't we?

I didn't stir, however, because my brain registered another thing as well – that the cry had come from downstairs, which meant that Emma had taken him down there, presumably to warm up one of the bottles she'd made up for him before going to bed.

But something was wrong. The crying wasn't stopping. I lay in bed listening for what seemed like several minutes, at first smiling wryly at the memory of those interminable night feeds – both mine and Riley's – but gradually becoming more and more agitated. How long did it take to warm a bottle? Not this long, surely. I glanced at the display on the alarm to find that it was approaching two-thirty. What on earth was she doing down there?

When the baby's cries were so plaintive I could almost feel his distress personally, I flipped the duvet from over my legs and dragged on my dressing gown, before shuffling out of the bedroom and trudging downstairs. Perhaps she was having a problem with the microwave or something.

The crying was coming from the front room, however – not the kitchen – so that's where I headed, and as I took in the scene I felt a wave of pure maternal anger. The baby was in his pram, screaming, kicking his little legs in frustration, while Emma, the sound conveniently muffled by a pair of earphones, was sitting cross-legged on the sofa, tapping away on – no, my eyes hadn't deceived me – my laptop! And at her side, I belatedly noticed, was a large measuring jug, half full of water, in which a bottle of milk was bobbing, presumably cooling after having been heated up too much.

Presumably now cooled, in fact. I snatched it up, wiped it on my dressing gown and placed the teat in Roman's open mouth, and while he sucked lustily – I held it in place for him as he fed – I turned my attention to Emma, who seemed almost completely oblivious. She'd seen me come in, of course – she'd even glanced at me – but she was doing that oh-so-teenagerish thing of finishing whatever she'd been doing – the furious typing of what was presumably some vital message – before deigning to pull out her earplugs and give me her full attention.

I stopped myself from picking up the baby. And it was hard. Though his hungry cries had by now been reduced to gulping sobs, this was no way for him to feed – he'd be gulping in as much air as nourishment – and it was only the insistent voice in my head, reminding me just how young and clueless (not to mention motherless) his mother was, that stopped me rounding on Emma in anger.

'Emma,' I said instead, keeping my voice low but firm, 'what's going on here? Surely you could hear Roman screaming? Even through those.' I gestured pointedly to the earphones.

She looked up at me, completely without guile. And then at her baby, as if nothing much was up with him. 'Oh, was it cool enough? I didn't realise. It takes for ever to cool down, milk does. And I know he fusses, but, look, he's fine now.' She paused then, as if unsure quite what to do with me, since it didn't look as if I planned on going anywhere any time soon. And then she seemed to decide I needed mollifying. 'It's all right,' she said, seeing me still standing

48

by the pram, feeding him. 'If you just roll his blanket up into a ball and prop the bottle up, he'll be fine. He can practically feed himself, that way.'

I was flabbergasted. He wasn't even five weeks old! Practically feed himself? 'Emma,' I said sternly, 'this bottle is almost stone cold. And a baby of Roman's age needs to be held while he's feeding and, equally to the point, what are you doing on my laptop at this hour of the night? What are you doing on my laptop at all?'

I could see from where I was that, as I'd thought, she was on Facebook, and was also aware that even now I didn't have her full attention. Her eyes kept flicking back to whoever she was messaging on screen.

'Emma!' I hissed again.

She sighed, betraying a distinctly adolescent irritation at the interruption. 'Oh, for God's sake, can't you chill, woman?' she fired back at me, causing me to be even more flabbergasted. 'I came down and warmed his bottle for him, didn't I? And would have fed him, too, if you hadn't come in and beat me to it. He's not going to die, you know, having to wait a few minutes. He's –' and then she stopped, abruptly, and burst out laughing.

Heaven knew, the last thing I wanted to sound like was the prissy Miss Jean Brodie character Kieron used to accuse me of sounding like whenever I used to tick him off, but that's exactly what I heard in my voice when I asked Emma quite what it was she seemed to find so funny.

But she evidently didn't. 'Oh, it's my mate,' she said, with one eye still on the screen. 'She's off her head on vodka, and she's having this major row with these two geeks on here. It's funny as.'

Words really did almost fail me now. But not quite. 'Well, I'm afraid I don't find anything about any of this remotely funny, Emma. This isn't a very good start, is it? Now kindly log off my computer, and come and sort your baby out, please. In the meantime I am going to switch the internet off, and you and I are going to discuss this in the morning.'

It nearly killed me to leave the room without picking up the baby, but I held firm and, as Emma watched me with the sullen eyes I absolutely expected, I left the room, climbed the stairs and crept as quietly as I could back into bed.

I couldn't sleep then. I tossed and turned all night, unable to settle, and though it might not have been conscious, with half an ear out for further baby-centred disturbances. And then, the following morning, without even thinking what I was doing, I did something completely out of character – I told a lie.

'I'm off now, love,' Mike said at seven as he placed my morning mug of coffee at the bedside. 'Well,' he went on cheerfully, 'that went well, eh? There was me worrying we'd be back to sleepless nights again – but nothing. Can't believe I never heard a peep!' He chuckled then. 'He's a lovely little fella, that one. They're both down there, by the way – Emma's busy changing him, and he's gurgling away, bless him. You know, I swear he's even watching the cartoons with her. I told her you'd been down once you'd had your coffee. Anyway, how about you?' he finished. 'Did you manage to sleep through?'

And I lied. 'Yes,' I said, nodding, 'I did. Right through.'

And I felt awful. I wasn't even sure why I'd lied to Mike, not really. Was it the idea that Hannah might just come and snatch Roman away without a by your leave? Was it because I felt so sorry for this poor motherless girl? Whatever the reason, I vowed then and there that it would not be – it mustn't be – the shape of things to come.

Chapter 5

What with the phone business and the computer business – not to mention the general night-feeding business – I had got out of bed that morning feeling somewhat heavy of heart. Emma hadn't even been with us for twenty-four hours yet, and already we'd been cast in the roles I least wanted – me as the stern deliverer of rules and regulations and her as the unwilling recipient. If ever there was a situation most likely to cement her position as a sulky teenager it was the one that I had no choice but to create: the speller out of ground rules on all fronts.

But perhaps that was going to happen anyway. Emma was just a child herself, after all. And though she wouldn't have to sit down and work through the list of points and privileges that was the basis of our specialist fostering programme, she perhaps did need to have certain things made clear.

Roman had gone straight to sleep after his morning feed, so I suggested Emma do likewise, and while she got her head down I got on the phone to Maggie about Emma's mobile.

'Oh, it's absolutely fine to let her have it,' she reassured me. 'Just as you would with any teen of her age. Unless you have good reason to think you shouldn't, obviously. Why – do you?'

'No, not really,' I said, swallowing the slight guilt I felt. 'We were just thinking of the circumstances and wanted to be sure, that's all, because she's a little older than the kids we normally have. What would constitute "good reason" in this case?'

'Oh, the usual,' Maggie said. 'If she's sitting chatting on it for long periods late at night, that sort of thing. In which case you'd obviously need her to leave it downstairs when she goes to bed.'

All of which constituted sound advice, I thought. And would be something with which I could reassure Mike when he got home. Though it wasn't late-night phone calls that I needed to have stern words about – it was the thing I'd neglected to mention to Maggie, the middle of the night sessions on my laptop. So that was exactly what I did, just as soon as she was downstairs.

'It won't happen again, Casey,' she promised plaintively. 'Honest it won't. I was just so lonely – it's scary being up in the middle of the night all by yourself, when everyone else is sleeping and everything, and now I don't have my iPod to listen to I just get so freaked out. An' I get so tired, I can hardly keep awake without anything to listen to. And I just saw it there – and you did say I could borrow it – and

Casey Watson

I just wanted to catch up with my friends. I've hardly seen any of them since Roman was born ...' She sighed. 'I just wanted to cheer myself up, that was all.'

Which left me with very little I could say, because, much as I knew it had been important to discipline her, at the same time my heart really went out to her. I remembered when Riley had been small and Mike had needed to be in the warehouse overnight for some reason and how frightened I'd been, left alone in the house with a tiny baby. And I'd been an adult, not a fourteen-year-old among strangers. I also remembered how when Kieron had been Emma's age he could hardly bear us being out for an evening, he'd get so twitched on his own, let alone a night.

And Emma had another dependent human being to think about now, too. Didn't matter that some might want to argue that it was self-inflicted. It would have been hard, and would still be hard for some time to come: hard to leave the usual childish things behind her, along with all her unencumbered friends. And such a shock to the system to one day be so carefree and the next have such an enormous responsibility.

No, I couldn't come down too hard on her because I did understand. I said so. 'But when I said you could borrow the laptop,' I pointed out, 'it was on the basis that you asked me first, wasn't it?'

She nodded glumly. But then brightened. 'But if I play my cards right I'll have my own soon anyway, won't I? So it won't be an issue, will it? And in the meantime I promise I'll only use yours if you say it's okay.'

'Which is never going to be in the middle of the night, I'm afraid,' I pointed out. After my chat with Maggie, this seemed fairly essential. 'But what about your iPod? What happened to it? Did it break?'

'No, I … well, actually, yes, kind of. It needed fixing and I never got it back off them after.'

'So should we follow that up?'

Emma shook her head. 'No, you're all right. No need. I don't think it was fixable.'

'Well,' I said, hearing the tell-tale bleat of a waking baby, 'I'm sure Riley or Kieron will be able to find you one – I think they both still have their old ones. No vouching for what's on them, of course – though I suspect you and Kieron share a taste in music – but he's a music whizz so I'm sure he can sort something out for you. That way, the nights won't seem so scary, eh?'

Which seemed to make Emma brighten. And as she skipped off to get Roman from his cot, I felt the heaviness lift. It hadn't been nearly as bad as I'd thought. Nor would it be, I decided, when I looked in on the pair of them an hour later. They were both curled on the sofa watching – of all things – a cartoon. And the thing that most struck me was that while Roman was sucking contentedly on his bottle, Emma, her hair once again scraped into a hurried and messy ponytail, was unthinkingly sucking her thumb. Who needed the most mothering in this scenario, I thought ruefully. The truth was that, actually, they both did.

* * *

Hannah was still going to be on her three-times-a-week phase for the first few weeks Emma was with us, and scheduled to come pretty much every other day. And by the time of the third visit, which was early the following week, I'd come to see a pattern had emerged. I wasn't privy to what had happened before she'd come to us, obviously, but I could see Hannah's visits really loomed in Emma's mind.

I didn't try to draw her out on the subject – I'd simply watch and see how things developed – but what was clear was that, like a nervous beginner anticipating their next driving lesson, Emma's mood grew increasingly anxious and raddled as the time of the next visit came around.

That the visits were necessary was not in dispute. As Roman's social worker, Hannah's responsibility was towards him. Where it was Maggie's job to oversee Emma's personal welfare, Hannah had no such professional remit. It was her job to look out for the interests of Emma's child, and if that meant parting him from his mother, then so be it. So I was well aware that a tough assessment was vital for the baby's welfare – I just hated seeing how much that stressed and upset Emma, who, knowing she'd be on show and scrutinised, presumably, would become negative and fatalistic and all fingers and thumbs. It almost felt like a self-fulfilling prophecy – a bit like being so nervous about your driving test that you shake so much you can barely drive. Except the stakes were way higher than being stuck with getting the bus. It was a cycle I was determined to break.

'Oh, Casey,' Emma wailed as the appointed hour grew nearer, 'can you help me find some clothes for him? I can't find anything decent to put him in!'

'Calm down,' I said. 'There's plenty of clean babygros in the airing cupboard. Just put him in one of those. He'll be fine.'

She wasn't to be mollified. 'Oh, I wish he'd been a girl. Girls are easy. You can put them in frilly stuff and make them look all pretty. Boys' clothes are shit. He always looks a mess.'

If it weren't for the need to give her a stern look about the swearing, I would have laughed out loud at this. It was just such a crazy thing to get in such a flap about. How things must have changed. But perhaps they hadn't – perhaps teen mums just cared because they were teens. And given the time teenage girls often spent caring about clothes shopping, perhaps it was just an extension of that.

'Emma, calm down,' I said again. 'Roman always looks beautiful. And you know, Hannah doesn't care a bit what he's dressed in. All that concerns her is that he's clean and he's healthy.'

I fished out a babygro and commanded her to put him in it. I was feeling guilty for having done too much that morning already – I'd given him his bath when he'd woken up, so she could get an extra hour's sleep. It had been such a little thing to do, but even so I knew I shouldn't have done it; particularly when she'd barely even noticed that I had done it – just whined about having had to get up for his night feeds and how unlucky she was to have a baby that still needed them, as if she didn't already have no luck at all.

She was still not dressed now, in fact, and Hannah would be arriving in half an hour. So, having delivered yet another lecture, about how all babies needed night feeds at this age – not to mention for some time to come – I suggested that now Roman was attired in his babygro she get on and make herself respectable too.

'Humph!' she huffed, tugging the belt of her dressing gown tighter round her. 'She can just take me as she finds me. She isn't my social worker, is she? I'm not doing anything till I've had something to eat.'

I went to make her breakfast almost on autopilot, really. After all, that was what I did – I looked after children. But even as I popped the slices of bread in the toaster, and reached for the hot chocolate, it occurred to me that, actually, I shouldn't be doing this. Emma didn't just have to prove to Hannah that she could look after Roman, she had to prove she could do so while still taking care of herself. After all, she was right – she wasn't one of the lucky ones, was she? If she'd been my child, I'd be there for her, helping her through the hard bit. If this had been Riley, that would have been exactly what I'd have done. Thank God it hadn't been, but saying it had, I'd be there for her, making her breakfast, supporting her, helping her through.

But that wasn't the case. Emma had no such support to rely on when she left me. She'd be on her own and, as such, she had to learn to survive.

I sighed heavily, as the reality of what was to come started sinking in. It was such a dilemma; I wanted to help her, but there was a clock ticking, loudly. In order to keep

Roman, she had to prove she could survive without help. She was being monitored and it was my job to collude with those doing that monitoring, which meant that if things went wrong – if the decision was reached that she couldn't be trusted to look after Roman – I would be a part of that decision-making process; a decision to part him from his mother. I couldn't remember the last time I'd felt so torn about a placement, or so emotionally on edge about what was the right thing to do.

I finished making the breakfast and took it in to her anyway. By now Roman had been relocated to his Moses basket – a surprise gift Mike had brought home a couple of evenings before. 'Save him having to be up in his cot upstairs all the time for his naps,' he'd explained. And I understood perfectly. Out of sight out of mind was the last thing that was required.

'Come on, Emma,' I said once she'd finished the first slice. 'Come on, get a move on!' She was flicking through the channels now, inertia kicking in. 'Get upstairs, get your-self showered, and get dressed, quick smart. You might not care what Hannah thinks, but I do. You need to show her that you can set a good example to your child, and lounging about watching TV in your PJs isn't one, in my book. Come on, take the rest of your toast up and get organised.'

She huffed again, and I was reminded that in the normal course of things she'd be in school, probably huffing about having to sit through double maths instead. 'A good exam-ple?' she spluttered. 'He's not even two months old! It's not like he's going to start copying me, is it? Christ!'

She stomped off then, slamming the door behind her for good measure, which made me flinch, expecting Roman to wake with a start and begin wailing, but he was obviously used to noise. He barely stirred.

Emma was still upstairs when Hannah arrived on the doorstep fifteen minutes later, looking a picture of smiling efficiency.

'Morning, Casey,' she said cheerfully as I ushered her over the threshold. 'Goodness, it's warm in here after the nip in the air out there. Had to ramp the heating up for our little man, I suppose?'

She shrugged her parka off as she went in, and cast around, looking for him.

'Exactly,' I said. 'Not ideal for a woman at my time of life, it must be said, but needs must, eh? Cup of coffee?'

'That would be lovely. Ah! There you are – look at you, all snug in your lovely basket!' She plucked Roman from his bed and turned back to me in one smooth movement. 'And where's our little madam today?' she asked.

It was nothing personal, but I didn't really like the way she called Emma 'our little madam'. It was the sort of term a mother might use affectionately for her own teenager, and, though it wasn't for me to say, in this context it just felt slightly inappropriate – as if she was already encouraging her to play that kind of role, despite Emma being a mother herself. It also riled me that Hannah was only young too and, though she was possibly the best social worker since the invention of sliced bread, had no personal experience of being a mum herself. (I'd checked.) Which didn't mean she couldn't do a brilliant job for Roman – some of the best midwives out there were childless, after all – but did mean it sat uneasily with me that she should slightly patronise Emma in that way. So I lied. I just didn't want to give her further fuel to think of Emma like that.

'She's upstairs sorting out the baby's laundry, I think,' I mumbled. 'I'll pop the kettle on then I'll nip up and tell her you're here.'

'Excellent,' said Hannah. 'Now, little fellow,' she said, turning back to Roman, 'how are you?'

Once I'd chivvied Emma down (having first, of course, briefed her) I left her and Hannah to it, and got on with doing a bit of laundry myself. I was out in the conservatory – a welcome addition Mike had made to the house not long after we'd moved in – hanging it on my airer when I heard the door go, and by the time I returned to the living room Emma was back in position on the sofa, Roman in the crook of one arm, remote in the other hand, TV on.

She glanced up. 'She said she'll see you Thursday,' she told me. 'And maybe phone you. Prob'ly to bitch about something else I'm doing wrong.'

'Wrong?' I asked. 'What did she say you were doing wrong?'

Emma pouted, seemingly lost for an answer. 'Nothing,' she admittedly finally. 'But she doesn't have to. I can just tell. She thinks I'm useless. "You should do this that way, you should do that this way. You should hold him like that, not like that –" She never stops.'

'Emma, that's not true.' I went and perched on the edge of the sofa. 'Sweetheart, honestly, that's not true. She just wants to help you learn how to look after him the best you can. That's what she's there for …'

'No she's not. She just wants to see how bad I am. So I don't know why she gets all uppity when I prove it to her – she should be pleased!'

'Love, that's not the case at all. Look, you really need to try and get along with Hannah. I know you don't like it, this whole assessment thing, but you have to take it seriously. It's not a game, you know. It *is* serious. So whatever you think about Hannah, you have to take it seriously.'

Emma's eyes glittered. 'Why?' she said angrily. 'What's the point? What difference is it going to make to anything? It's obvious they want him.' Her eyes flicked down to Roman. 'So you really think anything I do is going to make a difference?' She looked disgusted. 'They're short of babies, aren't they? You should know that. They've probably got some poor, sad, childless couple already lined up to have him. I know how it works. And if you don't you don't know anything!' She'd swung her legs around now, and was rising from the sofa, Roman in her arms still. 'Trust me, Casey, I know how it works. They're just waiting for me to fuck up enough for them to be able to whip him away.' She stomped to the door. Then spun round again. 'I'm not stupid!'

* * *

I left her alone. Left her alone for a good twenty minutes. I tidied the living room, gathering Roman's bits and bobs into one corner. Funny, I mused as I did so, how babies tended to spread. That was the start of a childhood, right there, the gradual tentacles of 'stuff' that reached all corners. Then, just as your house felt like it was full to bursting, there was this change – things started disappearing again, toys put away, stocks of plastic crockery dwindling. Childish presences became less and less, bedrooms became havens. And then, next, they'd be gone, the nest flown.

I folded the blanket Emma had discarded when she'd gone up to her bedroom. Was that what she really thought? And, more to the point, why was she so sure of it? Who'd planted that seed of mistrust in her mind and made her so sure of this conspiracy? Someone must have, for sure.

I went up quietly, suspecting that both mother and baby might be sleeping, but when I reached the top of the stairs I could hear a low sound. I hovered on the landing then, to catch what the noise was, and it was Emma. She was speaking and crying – I could tell because her voice had that unmistakable gulping quality. And what she was saying broke my heart.

'I wish,' she was whispering, 'I was a proper mummy, baby. I wish I was a proper mummy and that your daddy wasn't in jail. I wish I had a proper job like proper mummies do, friends who had babies so you had little friends to play with as well. I don't want to be alone. I don't want us to be alone.' I could hear her soothing him, going 'shhh, baby,

63

shhh go to sleep now'. Then she spoke again, and this time it was almost inaudible. 'I'm sorry,' she said, 'I'm useless, and I don't know what to do.'

So I would have to. I tiptoed back downstairs again.

Chapter 6

Kieron, my son, had recently qualified as a teaching assistant at our local primary school. He and his girlfriend, Lauren, had moved out of her parents' house and were now living in a small, rented flat, not far from our house. Whilst Lauren still had two jobs – splitting her time between working at a beauty salon and teaching dance to children – Kieron was now enjoying working full time in his new job in the learning support department.

I remembered him telling me only a few days ago about a mother and toddler group that one of his co-workers had set up in a local church. After hearing the sadness in Emma's voice as she had spoken to her baby, I decided I'd make some enquiries on her behalf. Mixing with other new mums might be just what she needed.

I was well aware that Emma was dreadfully lonely, and I knew that she regularly wrote to her boyfriend, Tarim. Almost every day she went out to post letters using stamps and stationery bought with money out of her allowance that was actually meant for Roman. This was another thing I had neglected to inform Hannah about. Emma received benefits to help her pay for baby formula, nappies and baby clothes, etc., but inevitably each Monday – she referred to this as 'pay day' – she would return from shopping with a new CD or magazine or a top for herself. I also had a suspicion that she was sending money in her letters to Tarim. I was determined, however, that she realise the importance of showing social services that she had her priorities right and I decided that I'd start accompanying her on her shopping days.

'Here,' I had said to her, just a few days earlier. I'd passed her a baby blue, padded jacket. 'Why don't you buy this for Roman? He'll look gorgeous in it and Hannah will be pleased to see it, I'm sure.'

I pushed it in front of Emma as she casually browsed through a rail of T-shirts in her size, and she gave it a quick glance.

'Nah,' she replied. 'Auntie Casey can buy it, though, if she wants.'

'Um, Auntie Casey has bought him quite enough, Emma,' I said in a huff. 'Perhaps if you spent less on flipping postage stamps, and more on Roman, you wouldn't moan so much about how he looked when you dressed him.' I glanced down at the pram, which I was pushing, and suddenly found myself getting annoyed as Emma just grinned back at me.

'Actually,' I said as I angled the pram handles in her direction, 'here, you take him for a while; I have some errands to run. I'll meet you back here at 12.30 and we'll go for some lunch.'

'Oh, Casey! You know how stressed I get lugging this bloody pram around. Can't you take him so I get a bit of "me" time?'

I was actually lost for words. I simply snorted and zipped up my coat. 'I'm off, love. I have things to do. I'll see you in an hour or so.' And with that I stomped out of the shop. 'Me' time indeed! I'd almost forgotten in such a short time what that felt like!

Now, though, after hearing her sobbing, I felt guilty. I phoned the mother and toddler group and asked for more information. They met twice a week and apparently the Thursday session had lots of very young mothers and babies. It sounded ideal for Emma. I listened as the woman who organised it all, Gemma, told me more. 'If you come along with her to the first session, you can sit and have a coffee with me while she settles in.'

'That's great,' I said. 'I'll have a chat with Emma then, and see if she's up for it. So you say Thursdays would be better?'

'Yes,' Gemma replied and then hesitated before explaining. 'It seems that by Thursday the girls tend to have no money left, so it's not completely altruistic of them. They get free milk, juice and snacks for the babies, and also as much tea, coffee and toast, etc., as they'd like for themselves. We also have a toy-borrowing system on a Thursday. The girls can pick up two or three toys to take home, and then return and swap them the following week.'

'Sounds great. I'll speak with her then, and hopefully we'll see you on Thursday.'

Feeling a lot better now that I was armed with good news, I went upstairs to tell Emma all about it. I smiled as I walked into her room. She had Roman laid on a blanket on the floor, and she was kneeling at his side blowing raspberries onto his stomach. Roman was shrieking with laughter each time he saw his mummy lean forward to get him again. Emma was laughing too, so I was pleased she had cheered up. 'Hey, you two. You look like you're having fun.'

'We are. We are, aren't we, my little man?' Emma said as she continued with her game. 'Sorry I was such a narky pants earlier, Casey. I just get a bit tired, that's all. And I miss Tarim. I really wish he was here with us.'

'I know, love. I do.' I wondered then if it was an opportunity to try to get Emma to talk a little about Tarim, but quickly decided against it. Better to approach the situation in hand first, while she was being reasonable. 'You'll just have to write him an extra-long letter when you're feeling lonely. I'm sure he won't mind you having a rant to him, will he?'

Emma looked up and giggled. 'I suppose not. And even if he does, it's not like he can do anything about it, is it? Mind you, if I got him annoyed he'd probably get me back by not phoning me or something. It's hard for him, Casey, being locked up and not knowing what I'm up to.'

'Up to?' I laughed. 'What, doing feeds and changing nappies?' I nearly added that he was having it easier than she was, in my opinion. But I didn't want to joke about him. I had my concerns about this boyfriend of hers. Every time she mentioned him I got the feeling that he must be quite controlling and it made me a little uncomfortable. I would definitely be bringing this up again. But for now I had to persuade her to join a group or two. Maybe then she wouldn't be so reliant on her boyfriend.

'Listen, love,' I said instead, 'I had an idea. A friend of Kieron's runs a brilliant young mum and baby group. There's loads of girls around your age and babies the same age as Roman. I think you'd really enjoy it.'

'Oh I don't know, Casey. I'm not really a group person. And girls my age don't usually like me. They all think I'm out to snag their boyfriends or something,' Emma said.

'Don't be daft. How could they not like you?' I decided to play it slightly differently. 'Also, imagine what Hannah would think? She'd be so impressed that you were doing something off your own steam for Roman's benefit.'

Emma thought for a moment and then stood up. 'You might be right, Casey. It would be like a slap in her face if I did it, wouldn't it? She'd have no reason to keep snooping around so much if I got my arse into gear, would she?'

This wasn't quite what I had in mind, but still, if it got her doing something. 'Well, she'd still have her usual visits, love, but she would have to record in her notes that you were showing initiative and trying to do something nice for Roman. You never know, you might meet some nice friends too.'

'Doubt it,' Emma grimaced as she spoke, 'and besides, I could never be mates with anyone that Tarim didn't know. He's good like that. He can read people like books. He always knows who would be right for me.'

I had to bite my lip to prevent myself from commenting. Maybe this was one of those instances where there were many little battles to be won before attempting the war. Maybe I needed to be more canny. Do some manoeuvring where all that was concerned.

'Right, that's settled then,' I said. 'I'll let Hannah know, and we'll go to the first session on Thursday. I'm looking forward to it.'

I was right. Hannah, who called the next day, was super-impressed that Emma had agreed to attend a group, and she told her how well she had been doing recently. After checking the baby over and speaking with Emma for a while, she asked if she could have a quick chat with me before leaving. We went through to the kitchen for a coffee.

'Just going through my list, Casey,' Hannah explained as she took a notebook out of her bag. 'It's nothing major, but I need to check how she's doing with Roman. The day-to-day stuff, and emotionally.'

She then went on to ask about Emma's routines and asked if I thought she was attending to Roman's needs, etc. In fact everything was fine until she asked, 'And what about this boyfriend? Has she admitted yet that he's the father?'

She watched me carefully as I shook my head. 'No. She talks about him at times, but she hasn't mentioned him being Roman's dad.' I felt slightly uncomfortable discussing this without saying that I thought Tarim was something of a control freak. But to be perfectly honest I didn't know this for sure. It was only my initial thoughts, and I felt I owed it to Emma not to bad mouth him until I understood more. Still, I wrestled with my motivation for holding back with Hannah. Was it because I wanted to protect Emma, or was it because I needed her to trust me enough to be able to confide in me? As soon as I realised it was the latter, it helped to strengthen my resolve. I needed Emma to see that I was in her corner, and speaking out now might just ruin things in that respect. If I could gain her trust, I could influence her choices in so many ways, and where Tarim was concerned that might be vital.

None of this, of course, was of real concern to Hannah. She was just there to see Roman was in a safe pair of hands. Something Emma still had to prove. So I was pleased to see Hannah closing her notebook for today. 'Is that it then?' I asked as she stood up.

'Yes, that's it for now. Let me know on Friday how the group meeting went and we'll take it from there. I will probably start cutting my visits down a little if Emma attends that regularly.'

Emma was delighted to hear that Hannah wouldn't be visiting so often and it set her mood for the remainder of that day. After she settled Roman down for his nap, I decided to broach the subject of Tarim once again. Mike had decided that he'd nip out to the fish and chip shop for supper and Emma was helping me butter bread and set the table. 'Oh, I hope he remembers to put the vinegar on at the chip shop, Casey, it tastes loads better than when you do it at home.'

I laughed as I realised that I thought the exact same thing. 'I know. How strange is that?' Then as casually as I could muster, 'Have you given any thought to what you'll do when Tarim gets released?'

Emma spun round to look at me and asked suspiciously, 'What do you mean?'

Clearly a way to go with that trust thing, I thought wryly. 'Well, he's obviously going to want to see Roman, isn't he?' I said. I noticed Emma blush and she averted her eyes. She began to chew nervously on her lip. 'Look, love. It's not my business, but I kind of guessed that he's the dad. I saw your photo at the side of your bed and they do look alike. But like I said, it isn't my business, and if you don't want to tell anyone I can understand that. You'll be scared that they might try to prosecute him, is that what it is?'

Emma nodded. 'Casey, I won't admit it to anyone. I really won't. Fair enough if you've guessed. Tarim can't say I've told you, but I'm sticking to my story. None of it is his fault. I knew what I was doing, and no one pushed me into anything.'

'I understand, love, and I know it's a sticky situation but, dad or not, if Tarim is to play a part in Roman's life, then social services will eventually need to know.'

'I don't see why!' Emma said. I could see she was getting worked up. 'All they need to know is that I can take care of my baby. Anything else is my business.'

72

'Right now, Emma, that's true. All I'm trying to say is that perhaps it would work in your favour if, later on, they can see that you are being open and honest. Don't worry about it yet though, love. We can cross that bridge when we get to it.'

I breathed a sigh of relief as I watched the words sink in without her getting upset. Drama averted, I busied myself making some hot drinks while Emma went up to check on Roman. I had opened the way up for a discussion but it was clear that she wasn't yet ready to confide in me with her plans for the future.

I was torn in reality. Part of me knew that Emma operated well knowing that she had Tarim in the background, and that speaking to him regularly and writing was holding them together and keeping her on an even keel. Though I didn't know her very well, I knew enough to know that it was his influence that kept her indoors with her baby. Other teen mums might have kicked up a fuss about not having time out with friends, but not Emma. She wanted Tarim to know that she was well and truly 'waiting' for him. Another part of me hated this. I could see that if Tarim was on the outside, this would be a very controlling relationship, and not a healthy one at all. But what could I do? I told myself that while he was away there was no harm being done, and in fact I was getting the best out of Emma. I just hoped I wouldn't live to regret my decision to allow it to continue.

Chapter 7

With Roman needing round-the-clock care and Emma being so young and vulnerable, it was perhaps no surprise that the next couple of weeks passed by in something of a baby-talc-scented blur. No surprise either that my focus was very much a tight one; the days revolving mostly around feeds, naps and washing, and the regular assessment visits made by Hannah, as well as trying to keep Emma positive and on track.

'Have I come to the right house?!' Riley asked when she came round for coffee the following Thursday. 'Does a Mrs Casey Watson actually live here?'

She looked around, her expression one of shock and stupefaction. 'Nope,' she said, poking her head into the kitchen and through lounge in turn. 'Nope again. No, I definitely have the wrong house.'

I shook my head while I scooped Jackson up for a cuddle. 'I have absolutely no idea what your mother is on about,' I told him.

'Fairy lights!' Riley clarified. 'Decorations! Trees! It's the first week in December and you don't yet have a single thing up. This has to be a record, mum. Has to be.'

Apart from visits to the letter-box, this morning was the first time Emma had been out without me since she'd been with us; she'd gone to the mother and baby group on her own, which was an important development. As was the fact that it was also the first time I'd had the house to myself since she'd come to us, too.

'Very funny,' I said, following Riley into the kitchen to make the drinks. 'Actually, your dad and I plan to go tree shopping this weekend. And the decorations are down, just not out. But they will be. You're right, though,' I admitted, 'I am way behind with everything. And haven't seen nearly enough of you, little man,' I finished, popping Jackson up on the kitchen counter in front of me. It was an unexpected treat to see him – normally he'd be in nursery. But with two teachers away from work with a tummy bug, they had made the difficult but probably sensible decision to ask those parents in a position to, to keep their little ones off as well. I began undoing his coat buttons, marvelling as ever at how quickly he seemed to be growing. He'd be three soon and, before we knew it, off to school like Levi, something I contemplated with very mixed emotions. On the one hand, it would be nice for Riley – she could then really get her teeth into her fostering – but at the same time, how had the time gone so fast?

'I'll get there,' I said. 'Well, eventually I will, anyway. It's incredible how quickly you forget just how time consuming a new baby is.'

'Two babies, don't forget,' Riley pointed out. 'You're looking after both of them, Mum. Don't forget that. How's Emma getting on anyway? Is she coping any better now?'

'Definitely. I have every confidence in her,' I said, and perhaps a touch more forcefully than I intended. I wasn't speaking to Hannah, after all, was I? Riley knew the score. I sighed then, almost automatically. It didn't matter if Emma passed muster for Hannah and social services with flying colours. She still had the next bit to get through, didn't she? And with little in the way of emotional support, bar a dubious-sounding boyfriend, currently in jail. That would be the difficult bit, in comparison. I gave Riley a rueful smile as I put Jackson down and popped his coat over a chair back. 'Though when you look into their future …,' I went on, 'well, all I can see is hurdles. I just hope she's going to have the wherewithal to climb over them. She's just so young. And it's not helped by knowing that the boyfriend's waiting in the wings, either. I haven't even clapped eyes on him and I worry about what's going to happen. It's not the greatest situation to be born into, is it? To have a convicted drug dealer as a dad.'

Riley nodded. 'But who knows? It might become the making of him, mightn't it? Well, once it's out there that he is the dad, at any rate. Might persuade him to shape up and take responsibility. Do you know when he's coming out of prison?'

'No,' I said. 'Maggie doesn't know. Just not yet.'

And, I thought, long may that state of affairs continue. I had little to go on, but my hunch was that when that day happened things might just get a whole lot more complicated.

But with the twin preoccupations of Tarim and Christmas, I'd perhaps taken my eye off the ball where Emma's emotional state was concerned. Up to this point, there was one subject that Emma and I hadn't discussed: her mother, and the role she'd played in her life. Which was fine – if a child didn't want to talk about their family background, then so be it. Though we always made it clear we were happy to listen, we were not there to interrogate them or, for that matter, formally counsel them. Our job was to take care of them, full stop. Though, obviously, sometimes prompted by a family photo, or a recollection, a conversation would be sparked and a child would want to talk to us – and in that case, our care of them would naturally include listening to their problems and helping them process how they might deal with them. It also meant being honest about hearing things that were potentially actionable. If a child confided they had been abused, for example, I had to make it clear to them I would need to share what they had told me with people who might be able to help. This didn't always go down as well as might be imagined. If a child had been sworn to secrecy, for example, by the adult or adults in question, the feeling that they'd told on them could be every bit as distressing for a child as the abuse itself.

I didn't think this applied to Emma, but I obviously did know she was estranged from her mother, and as there's nothing like the approach of Christmas to concentrate the mind when it came to family, Emma's mum and what might happen was definitely on my mind. Given our line of work, Mike and I had now spent several Christmases that included children who'd barely known the joy of spending one with a family of their own or, if they had, one blighted by abuse or neglect. We still did – the first child we ever fostered, Justin, now a strapping lad of seventeen, still spent Christmas Day with us every year. Usually this happened at Riley's since she was now the one with the little ones, but this year, because of our current situation, we had decided that the annual family feast would be at our house. I couldn't wait. There was nothing like having a baby around at Christmas.

But not everyone felt the same as I did, clearly, and it was on a chilly morning about half-way through December when both Emma and I were about to find that out. It was feeling slightly more Christmassy now. There was no sign of actual snow yet, though the air was certainly cold enough and when I'd put my head outside the door to grab the milk I thought it might have snowed, the garden was so completely frosted with silvery-white. The post was slightly later, landing with a pleasingly hefty thump just as I was clearing away the breakfast things and Emma had gone into the living room to change Roman's nappy. This was a regular event since the tree had gone up as he loved staring up at it – me being me I had the fairy lights going all day.

I went out into the hall wondering how many Christmas cards had landed. I'd spent an enjoyable evening a few nights back doing mine, and was looking forward to catching up now with old friends. I'd had a varied life, job wise, and it was nice to stay in touch with all the people I'd worked with along the way.

The scattered pile was made up of the usual collection of envelopes; the obvious Christmas cards, the obvious bills, the obvious junk mail and flyers, but as I riffled through, pulling the cards to the top so I could open those first, I noticed one in the pile addressed to Emma. Not that there was anything unusual in Emma getting letters; she had been receiving them almost every other day since she'd arrived with us – something Maggie didn't have a problem with – but this one was different: it didn't have the HMP prison stamp on it. So not from Tarim, this one. I wondered who might have sent it. As in the case of all children in care, it was important to monitor who they had contact with. I looked again at the envelope. The handwriting was tiny and spidery, meandering in a gentle downward slope across the front; the hand was distinctive, too, and right away something told me it was an older, rather than a younger hand.

'There's a letter for you, love,' I said, taking my small haul into the living room.

Emma was kneeling by the changing mat, just doing the poppers up on Roman's vest. She was becoming practised now, handling him so much more confidently and easily.

'Really?' she said, turning to smile, her ponytail flicking round as she did. Her hair was looking better as well, I thought, now she was over that debilitating early period.

As was her skin, which was getting some colour back at last.

I handed the letter to her. It wasn't thick – at most a couple of pages, probably only one. And not a card. It wasn't stiff enough for that.

Nevertheless, she seemed to think it might be.

'Oh my God,' she said, as she studied it. 'Oh my God, it's from my mum, Casey! Shit, it's been months …' She peeled the corner of the flap. 'Like, months and months. I bet it's for Christmas. I bet it's a Christmas card or some money or something!' She finished ripping the flap open and began tugging out the contents.

'That's nice,' I said, kneeling down alongside her and tickling Roman's tummy.

'She always does this,' Emma qualified. 'When she's been through one of her episodes and that. Says sorry and stuff …'

She tailed off then and unfolded the sheet of paper inside.

I don't know if I believe in a sixth sense – not really – but as she began reading I had this sudden jolt of anxiety about what the contents might say. I had no reason to – even with the history between them; this was Christmas, after all. And at Christmas people sometimes become better people, at least temporarily – or at least feel guilty about not having been. And given that history, perhaps Emma's mother was having one of her 'good' periods, and, damaging though they undoubtedly had been and would be, children always kept the faith. They almost never gave up on hope.

But I had been here before, with other kids, and perhaps that was what had prompted it; that kind of heart in mouth sensation I knew so well.

And as soon as I saw Emma's expression change from one of delight to one of despair, I knew the feeling had been right, however much I wished it hadn't been.

'What is it, love?' I asked gently, but she was too absorbed in whatever she was reading to hear me. I watched her face crumple and saw tears begin welling. 'Sweetheart …' I prompted. Emma turned to me then and, hand trembling, she passed the letter.

'Here,' she said brokenly, 'read it yourself. The bitch! The fucking bitch!' She stood up, leaving Roman gurgling on the carpet, and walked over to the window, furiously wiping at her tears. 'Why, Casey? Why does she hate me?'

I had already read the first line – 'I suppose you think you're so clever, don't you?' – and, tearing my eyes from Emma, braced myself for the rest. And perhaps Emma was right – what I saw written there could only be described as hate mail, and it broke my heart that a mother could speak to her child like this.

Dear Emma

I suppose you think you're so clever, don't you?
Leaving me when I needed you the most and choosing that evil bastard and his spawn over me. You think you can just desert me and then send the social round, begging me to take you back? Well, no. Not this time, girl, you've really messed up. I've finished with

you now, and to think that you are actually a mother, what a laugh! You aren't fit to wipe that baby's arse!

Don't worry though, Emma, you won't have him for long. The social will have him off you in a breath when they see how completely useless you are. If I've got anything to do with it, he'll be put into care and you'll never see him again. That way you can get on with it, play at being a grown up with that junkie dealer. The next letter you get will probably be addressed to the next prison cell to his. Won't that be a laugh? Anyway, fuck you and your kid. You've been a weight around my neck since the day you were born.

Mum

I had to take a gulp of air as I folded the letter up and looked at Emma, and I realised I'd been holding my breath. She was watching me now, waiting for a reaction, I suspected, and I gave her one. I smiled at her, weakly.

'Do you want to talk about it, love?' I asked her.

'What's to talk about?' she fired back at me. 'I think she made herself pretty clear. That, Casey, is my mother for you.'

I picked Roman up from where he was kicking about and placed him in his Moses basket with his bunny-rabbit rattle.

'Come on,' I said to Emma as I sat on the sofa and patted the space next to me. 'Sit down for a minute and let's just think about it. It sounds to me like your mum is very angry at someone or something, but I can't believe that she won't regret writing all this.'

Emma, sobbing freely now, sat down heavily beside me. And as she crossed her legs under her and lowered her head into her hands, it really struck me just how young she was. 'She won't regret it, Casey,' she said, lifting her head again. 'She never does. She might forget it, and never mention it again, but regret? No, that's not her style. She's never happy unless she's upsetting somebody.'

'She's said things like this before, then?' I asked. I'd seen all sorts in my time but some things never changed – like just how appalled I felt that a mother could hurt her daughter like this.

Emma sniffed and then gave a harsh laugh. 'That's tame compared to some of her motherly rants, trust me! I don't know what they've already told you, but she's sick in the head.'

'You mean mentally ill?' I asked.

Her voice was full of bitterness. 'And the rest! She calls it depression and has tablets for it and everything, but soon as she starts to feel better she quits them and says she doesn't need them any more. Even accuses the doctor of trying to poison her and stuff. That's when she turns into a complete *Loony Tunes*.' She nodded towards the letter I was still holding. 'She's probably off the pills now. I'm sick of it, Casey. She's been like this ever since I was a kid.'

I wasn't surprised she was sick of it. It was clear that she'd become no more used to her mother's breathtaking cruelty than I had. She wiped the back of a hand across her eyes.

'She sometimes used to forget I even existed. Would piss off somewhere for hours on end and forget to buy food and stuff. Then after days of me begging her to take her tablets, she'd suddenly spend every penny we had on a new TV or a big bike for me or something.' She turned to look at me. 'Honestly, she's mad!'

I listened in growing amazement. What a childhood Emma had endured. It must have been so hard for her growing up with this see-saw existence. What a life sentence it must have been – still was, in fact – the business of having a mother whose life was dominated by bouts of depression.

'Well at least you know that it's a sickness, love. I know it must still hurt, and God knows how I would feel in your shoes, so let's hope she gets better again, and soon.'

Emma stood up, and her expression seemed to say that, actually, she'd heard this before – many times before. 'I won't hold my breath,' she said flatly. She then glanced over at Roman, who was now fast asleep in the Moses basket. 'Is it okay if I get a shower while he's quiet?' She sighed as though resigned to her fate. She looked suddenly worn out. I wondered what effect her mother might imagine her note would have on her. Did she even think that clearly? Think at all?

'Course you can, love,' I said. 'Go on – go and have your shower. I'll see to him if he wakes up.'

I watched her go, noting the dejected slope of her narrow shoulders, and weighing the single sheet of cheap paper in my hand. This was terrible. I needed to find out more about the poor girl's history. And, now I thought about it, how come her mother had been given our home address? I gave it five minutes, then got on the phone to John Fulshaw.

Chapter 8

January is never my favourite month – is it anyone's? Such a depressing come-down from Christmas and New Year, it's the sort of gloomy month that could do with being cancelled – and the whole 'twelfth night, decorations down' thing with it. If I ruled the world, I mused, as I drove the short distance to Kieron's, I'd decree that all fairy lights stayed in position at least till the clocks all went forward.

But it wasn't just the short days and long nights that were getting to me; it was Emma, who had seemed so stuck in glumsville since Christmas that if I didn't know her problems were way too big to be addressed by quick fixes, I'd have gone and ordered her one of those light boxes off the internet. It was mid-January now and the mother and baby group were meeting again, but I'd been unable to coax her out to attend the day's session – or come to Kieron's with me either, for that matter. I almost offered to take the baby with me but pulled back from actually saying it; much as I knew she could use the sleep (or, more likely, the time on the laptop) it wasn't the sort of thing I was supposed to be doing, so in the end, telling her I'd only be gone an hour or so and suggesting she could perhaps write to Tarim, I left her and little Roman to it.

'I can't say I blame her,' Lauren said, leaving the flat just as I was arriving. She was off to teach her first dance class of the New Year, and seemed to be wearing three woolly scarves all at once, one of them almost the same shade of pink as her nose. 'If that church hall is anything like as cold as the community centre I work in,' she laughed, 'she's made a shrewd decision staying put in the warm.'

I knew that, and I didn't want to press her to socialise. She was obviously still hurting badly from the memory of her mother's cruel invective, and it didn't matter how much she had told us that she knew it was just the drink talking and that she'd become used to it over the years – I'd yet to meet a child who didn't crave a parent's love, or hope that one day, just one day, they might get some. She'd also been particularly quiet on the subject of Tarim, and I had this persistent itch about what might be going on there. I had no grounds for my worries – well, no more than I'd had since day one – but she'd just been so uncommunicative since the day she'd had her mum's letter, and though I was pleased in one way that everything we were doing was so baby-centred, I felt frustrated about the wall there still was between us. Still, chatting with Kieron always made me feel a bit better, and though I'd popped round to see how he was doing in his new job I always valued his refreshing brand of black or white insight.

'It's much harder with teenagers, isn't it?' was Kieron's sage comment, once we'd waved Lauren off and made coffee. 'I remember you saying that to me once. It's always stuck.'

'Has it?' I smiled. My son looked so grown up all of a sudden, his blond bum-fluff replaced by a coarse mat of designer stubble. He was growing more like Mike by the day. 'So what did I say exactly? I'm assuming you were on the receiving end of one of my moans after doing something despicable – yes?'

'I wasn't, actually,' he said. 'It was when we were watching something on the telly about teenage runaways, and I remember you saying that the teenage bit was the worst bit. That everyone always said that the hard part was the first part, with all the sleepless nights and terrible twos and so on, but that, actually, that wasn't true.'

I grinned at him. 'I did?'

Kieron nodded. 'You said it was hard because with little ones you could almost always solve their problems, and that with teenagers you couldn't – that a lot of the time all you could do was support them through them.'

I didn't recall the conversation, but I wasn't surprised Kieron had. He was good at remembering things, and very often verbatim. And I didn't doubt I'd said that, and I could probably pinpoint when, too. It would have been when I was working in pastoral care in our big local comprehensive – running what was informally (not to mention infamously) called The Unit – and usually filled with a number of adolescents who had the sort of family and social problems that didn't lend themselves to fixes, quick or otherwise. It was one of the reasons I went into fostering in the first place, so I could better provide support, one on one.

And this one was proving intractable. The fact was that Roman was still a baby and, grim though the thought was, if he was taken from Emma he'd barely even remember her. He'd more than likely get placed within a lovely foster family, and, given his age, be adopted in no time. No, it was Emma who needed my support here, if she was going to be allowed to hang on to him. And if they didn't let her – if they took him from her – what then? Kieron was right; I had been clear on what I thought was the most challenging part of parenting. But I don't think any amount of sage advice could have prepared me for what I found when I got home an hour or so later.

Even before I put my key in the front door I could tell something was wrong. Babies have all sorts of different cries, as any mother soon learns, all of them transmitting a different need. As with Inuits, and their endless reams of words to describe snow, a mum soon gets used to identifying all the different ways their infant tries to communicate their needs; the ones that say I'm hungry, the ones that say I'm tired, the ones that say, 'Leave me alone! I'm overstimulated! Just put me down and let me lie here …'

I knew the nature of the cry that I could hear from the other side of the frosted glass. It was a distressed cry, but at the same time had a very specific quality. It was the cry of a distressed baby who was also exhausted from long crying. The sort of cry that baby manuals tell you to try and ignore in the small hours, when you're trying to get them to settle themselves and sleep through the night. But a baby of Roman's age shouldn't be left to cry like that, ever. He was a scant four months old, bless the little mite.

I twisted my key in the lock and called out to Emma as I stepped inside. Fallen asleep, was my guess, and I exhaled in exasperation, knowing precisely what I'd find when I got up to her bedroom – Emma spark out, with her earphones in, oblivious to Roman's wailing, the sound drowned out by whichever cool R&B star was currently flavour of the month.

It wasn't surprising, then, that I got no response to my call, and, shrugging off my coat, I made my way up the stairs. But when I went into Emma's bedroom, where Roman was indeed lying in his cot crying, there was no sign of Emma herself. I scooped him up, rubbing his back and nestling him tight against my neck, which he nuzzled against, rooting for milk.

'I haven't got anything for you, lovely,' I whispered, feeling an automatic stab of anger and irritation that he had been left to get into this state. That's what a baby's cry did to you. Put you all out of sorts. 'Where's mummy, eh?' I asked him as I carried him out of the room again, his sobs, though no less anguished, at least becoming quieter, now he was at least being cuddled and rocked.

But now Roman was a little quieter I could hear something else – a new noise. It was the sound of retching and it was coming from the bathroom. I crossed the landing in two strides. The door was partly open and as soon as I reached it, it was obvious what was happening, as I could immediately see a pair of feet, encased in fluorescent yellow socks. I pushed the door open further to see Emma kneeling over the toilet bowl, heaving, though nothing much seemed to be coming out.

'Emma?' I asked, my previous concern for Roman being supplanted by a rush of sympathy for her instead. 'Emma, love,' I said again. 'Are you all right?'

Her response was to let out a long anguished groan, which turned almost immediately into a coughing fit. And then into a flood of shoulder-shuddering tears. Since I couldn't look after both of them, I took an executive decision, grabbing a couple of big bath towels off the rail and throwing them in the bath, then laying a startled Roman unceremoniously onto them. I then turned my attention to Emma, whose tears had been truncated by another bout of retching, even though all she was bringing up was bile. I pulled her hair from her neck, feeling the clamminess of her pale skin. 'Love,' I said, confused, there having been no inkling she was feeling queasy when I left her, 'when did this start? Have you been feeling sick for long?'

She reached for some loo roll, then shook her head miserably. And then, as I watched, it seemed to crumple in on itself all over again. 'Oh Casey,' she wailed. 'I took a load of aspirins …'

'*Aspirins*?'

She nodded wretchedly. 'I took an overdose. I just wanted to … I just couldn't … but now I don't, and so I tried to …' She trailed off then, seemingly incapable of continuing, her eyes swimming. 'Oh, *God*, Casey!' she said next. 'Am I going to *die*?'

I called an ambulance and Mike, in that order. Emma was hazy about how many pills she'd taken, so though she thought she'd sicked up quite a lot (she'd opted for the traditional salt-water trick) there was no knowing how many had already been absorbed once she'd done that, and as one of the main 'musts' I remembered from training was that I must never take any chances, I wasn't about to try and make a judgement about it either. Instead I got a plastic bowl and then relocated from her station by the toilet bowl to a chair at the kitchen table so that I could keep an eye on her while I made up Roman's bottle.

Roman, by now exhausted, had fallen asleep in the bath, so that's where I'd left him while I helped Emma downstairs. I knew he'd wake again soon enough and begin howling. And I needed to be ready for him – whatever happened now I knew we'd probably be headed off to hospital. I didn't remember everything off the top of my head, but one thing that had stuck when it came to aspirin overdoses was that, even if the patient appeared to have got most of it out of their system, there still needed to be a period of medical observation. Which, given the time, probably meant a night in hospital.

Mike was back first. 'Never rains in this house, does it?' he quipped wryly as I shuffled him straight upstairs to change out of his work clothes and retrieve the baby. I knew I'd also need to get some night things and toiletries together for Emma, but I could do that once Mike was back down and feeding Roman. In the meantime, or so the remnants of my first-aid course seemed to be telling me, the important thing was to keep Emma upright and conscious. Though this was clearly no time for light-hearted small talk. Nor did she seem to want it to be.

'I can't believe I did it, honest I can't,' she said, as I bustled round getting teats from the steriliser while trying at the same time to keep an eye on how she was looking. I was pleased to see that she had a slightly better colour now she was up off the floor, though her skin still looked damp. She was crying still, but not convulsively now – just a steady stream of miserable tears, which she mopped intermittently with sheets of kitchen roll.

'That makes two of us,' I said, just stopping short of asking her any of the questions that were teeming in my head. Had she planned to do this? Had she just been wait-ing for her opportunity? Because chief among the answers I was after was where precisely she'd got all the aspirins. We never used them. In keeping with most people with youngsters in the house, we had ditched them when it came out that, albeit in rare cases, giving them to children under twelve could be fatal.

Which meant Emma had either had them all along or had been secretly stockpiling them with just this eventuality in mind. It was a depressing thought – potentially a whole other can of worms – and it made me more angry at her mother than ever. I knew alcoholism was a disease and needed to be treated accordingly, but I couldn't help thinking how much I'd like to see Emma's 'sick' mother witness what her daughter had just tried to do.

But it seemed I was way off beam. *Way* off.

'I just wanted to *show* him …' she continued. 'Just punish him. Just make him realise …' her voice was rising now. 'And all I've done is –' she broke down again, but she didn't need to finish. I knew what she was thinking about. About her child.

But him? She had said *him*. 'What, you mean Tarim?' I asked her.

Her voice hardened now. 'Yes,' she said. 'Of course I mean Taz! The one fucking person I thought I'd could fucking rely on! But, oh, what a surprise – I *fucking* can't!'

Emma grimaced then, just as I was taking all this in. 'Oh, God!' She grabbed the bowl. 'I think I'm going to be sick again …'

At which point the doorbell rang, Mike appeared, and Roman recommenced his screaming. Mike was right. No rain in our house. It *always* poured.

I had made more visits to our local A&E than I cared to remember, so after Emma had been examined, reassured she wasn't about to die and given some medication to counteract the acid, I steeled myself for the long stint ahead.

No, she wasn't going to die – in all probability she would need a 'gastric lavage' to be on the safe side, but that was that – but now we were on a road without turn-offs. The paramedics – two lovely guys, one very young, one close to retirement – were as patient and upbeat as they always were, but even through their smiles I could see them taking in an all too familiar situation. They'd seen most things, done most things and above all knew one main thing – that it would be a very long-drawn-out evening, as, once in the care of the NHS, as she was now, procedures had to be carried out and protocols followed. Still, I thought, as I climbed into the ambulance with one very disconsolate and whey-faced fourteen-year-old, at least this might be the start of some proper conversation between us.

And I was right. 'I feel so bad, Casey,' Emma said as we pulled up outside the ambulance entrance of A&E and the paramedic jumped down to sort out the ramp. 'Will Mike be all right? You know – with Roman? Will he manage okay on his own?'

I gave her a smile. 'He'll manage *fine*,' I reassured her. 'Why on earth would you think he wouldn't?'

She shrugged. 'I dunno. It's just – well, it's not really men's stuff, is it? Looking after babies and that.'

I didn't know quite where to start with *that* one. And perhaps I shouldn't. Get me on that one and I could have a field day. So I didn't. It was only another one of Tarim's ridiculous pronouncements, no doubt. 'Mike's an expert,' I told Emma firmly. 'So don't you worry, okay?' I leaned across and drew an arm around her shoulder, pulling her in for a hug. 'At this moment, the important thing is to make sure *you're* all right, okay.'

Which only served to make her start crying again. 'If he just hadn't *ignored* me,' she cried into my chest. 'I've messed everything up big time now, haven't I?'

If Emma was beginning to regret the impetuosity of her actions, I was beginning to feel a chill wind of inevitability blowing with increasing force around my plastic chair in A&E. I knew exactly what would happen now, every step of the process; and as we went straight from triage to a side room to another examination to doing the blood tests (to check her blood for toxins), I also knew the next part, given that this was a suicide attempt, would be an admission to the ward and the allocation of a kindly attentive nurse, who would gently probe Emma to see why she had done it.

In the meantime, I had left Mike with instructions to phone the crisis team at social services. The hospital would obviously be obliged to call them as well, but it was important that we make our own report, to cover ourselves legally. Then it was a case of ticking the correct boxes. After a night on the ward, with checks of her vital signs every four hours, Emma would greet the morning and a concerned team member simultaneously, and in all likelihood be immediately referred to the Child and Adolescent Mental Health Service. This was not *just* box-ticking either. With social services *in loco parentis* it was vitally important that they assess her thoroughly to see how much, if any, danger Emma posed to herself. Would she need further psychiatric treatment, either as an in-patient or out-patient, or would she be considered safe to be returned to me?

But before that, I had news to impart to various people myself. When I left the hospital, at around 9 p.m., it was with the grim realisation that I would spend the next half hour on the phone to John Fulshaw, then Maggie and finally Hannah, all of whom, understandably, would be concerned.

'So she's being referred to CAMHS?' asked Hannah.

'Yes,' I confirmed. 'I think that's the plan.'

'Good,' said Hannah, who had to be properly filled in, obviously. And who was currently in the middle of making an assessment of whether Emma was considered fit to be Roman's mother.

Chapter 9

I woke up the next morning feeling guilty. Not so much about what had happened as what I had said about what had happened. I knew this incident would affect Emma's progress report badly and as a result I had chosen my words carefully. Her 'cry for help' (a clichéd expression, but an accurate one in this case) had been directed not at her mother but at her absentee boyfriend – it was him she'd wanted to punish by taking that overdose of aspirins. But that wasn't quite how I'd described it. Even though I knew differently – or, at least, I thought I did – I'd made much more of the business of Emma having been devastated by her mother's letter, hoping that Maggie and Hannah would agree with me that it was a terrible thing to receive and might push any already fragile teen over the edge. Perhaps then they'd feel more sympathetic. And perhaps less convinced than they might be that with Tarim pulling strings – as he seemed to be doing – Roman's future with Emma needed serious thought.

Which put me on dangerous ground. Suppose they accepted things, and let Emma keep Roman, and then her boyfriend turned out to be the father from hell? How would I feel about everything then? That wouldn't happen, I told myself sternly. I wouldn't let it. If he came out of prison and I had the tiniest concern, I'd share it, whatever the consequences for Emma. I just hoped it wouldn't come to that.

I'd been told to call at ten the next morning, to establish whether Emma was going to be discharged, and was pleased and relieved to be told that she was. Yes, she'd looked rueful and reasonably calm when I'd left her the previous evening. She'd been seen by someone from social services and they were going to try and get her CAMHS appointment scheduled but, in the meantime, she was apparently good to go. Mike had taken the day off so we could go up and collect her together, and I was pleased. It wasn't a big thing, but presenting a united front was just one of the ways we could show her our support. It also made it easier to bring Roman.

But though she cooed when she saw him I could tell she was preoccupied. Her eyes were red, too, from what I judged was recent crying. And a gentle enquiry, while Mike showed off Roman to the nurses, revealed she had been; she was still extremely upset about Tarim.

'I hate it when he does this to me,' she said, when I asked her how she was feeling. 'I hate him!' She pulled her few bits from the locker and threw them on the rumpled bed, where I'd placed her pink holdall for the purpose. 'An' I know why he does it, too. He's such an S.H.I.T., Casey! He ignores me for ages almost as if he's trying to push me away from him, just so that when he does get back in touch with me he can start giving me grief about what I've been up to.'

It struck me as a strange kind of logic, but she was obviously on a roll now. I'd barely opened my mouth to answer when she started up again. 'I know what his game is. He'll ring – in the end he will – and then it'll be all "Where've you been going? Who've you been seeing?" and when I swear blind I've been nowhere it'll be all "Oh, yeah, I'll *bet*. It's not like I'd know, is it? Stuck in here rotting." He never believes me, Casey. *Never*.'

I folded Emma's crumpled pyjama bottoms and added them to the bag. What I wanted to say to her – or, more specifically, have her point out to him – was *well, whose fault was that, matey*? But that wouldn't be helpful. So instead I said, 'Come on, now. That's just silly, love. You should tell him that if he were to use some of his money actually phoning you, then he would know where you were, wouldn't he?', but as soon as I said it I realised I was actually condoning his ridiculous reasoning – more or less telling Emma that staying in and waiting for his phone calls was the answer when, actually, the reverse was true!

I zipped up the bag and rethought what I didn't say originally. 'Love,' I said, 'I know it can't be nice for Tarim being stuck in prison, but you didn't put him in there, did you? And he really has no business thinking the worst, or any excuse for punishing you – not that you deserve to be punished because you've done nothing wrong – by purposely ignoring your calls and letters.' I looked over to where Mike and Roman seemed to be completely derailing the smooth running of the ward – there were eight or nine nurses clustered around them now.

'Emma,' I said, 'Tarim needs to learn to trust you. You are doing nothing wrong, and if he loves you like you say he does, he'll want you to have a life while you're waiting for his release. I know you've got Roman to think about but that doesn't mean you should be sitting at home every day and night; that's no good for anyone, least of all a teenage girl. He's going to have to learn to trust you, and you need to learn not to be so reliant on his texts and calls. That's half the problem; he knows that's exactly what you *are* doing, so he has you where he wants you. But is that what you really want for yourself? You need friends, Emma. *Everyone* needs friends. He might mean everything to you, but he isn't the be all and end all, and nor should he be. And he needs to know that – you've got to stand up to him, be a bit more independent.'

There was a sullen silence, which I took to mean she was digesting my words, albeit reluctantly. I ploughed on. 'What about that young girl you lived with when you had Roman? Are you in touch with her at all? Why don't you get back in touch with her again? You must be missing her.'

Emma looked at me so intently that I thought she was going to kick off, to berate me for telling her what to do, who to see, and for 'dissing' her precious Tarim. But she didn't. She thrust her arms into the sleeves of her jacket and narrowed her eyes. 'Kemma?' she said, laughing entirely without humour. 'You think I want to speak to her again after she and her mum threw me out? Do me a favour! She's no friend of mine any more.'

'Ah, I see …' I started saying, but she obviously hadn't finished. 'You know what?' she said then. 'You're right, actually, Casey. Tarim really thinks I'm some kind of numpty, doesn't he? Sat at home, bringing the kid up, while he does nothing. Well, I'm not going to be,' she sniffed. 'Not any more!'

And, with that, she snatched up the holdall and began heading off out of the ward, leaving a bemused Mike and Roman and me following in her wake, grabbing the CAMHS appointment letter from the staff nurse as we went.

By the time we got home, Emma seemed in a much less pugilistic mood and I was pleased to see that Roman finally seemed to be clawing back most of her attention once again. And with everything calm, Mike decided to head into work for the afternoon after all. 'No sense in using up a half day's holiday unnecessarily,' he said, 'since I'm no longer required to hold the baby.'

I kissed his cheek and said we'd see him later. No sense in jumping in and telling him that what I had in mind involved exactly that, well, sort of. Not till he'd had his tea, at any rate.

'So, I was thinking,' I was saying to Maggie Cunliffe, not twenty minutes later, 'I know the plan was that we weren't going to make one till it's settled that Emma's definitely keeping Roman, but do we have to wait? Because I was thinking that perhaps the sensible next step would be for Mike and me to become Roman's official child minders. You know, just like regular child minders, looking after Roman on a day-to-day basis, so that Emma can resume her education.'

'You two?' Maggie said. 'Are you sure about this?'

Emma was out of earshot, upstairs changing the baby before putting him down for an afternoon nap, but I still kept my voice low as I answered. 'Yes, I am. I think it's important that she gets back into some sort of school environment. I'm really concerned at how isolated she seems to be from her peers. From what she's told me and what I've read, she's not attended school properly in something like eighteen months now, which I know is partly due to the pregnancy but that *is* only a part of it. It seems to me it's mostly been to do with Tarim telling her who she can and can't hang out with. Which isn't healthy, is it? She needs to have friends her own age to offload to. Not to mention needing some sort of focus and routine. If she's to support a baby – not to mention build up her own self-esteem – then she needs a life *beyond* the boyfriend. And right now – with him out of the picture for a bit – seems the perfect time to try and set that up.'

'Well, that does seem to make sense,' Maggie agreed. 'In theory, at least. But it would only work if Emma committed to it properly. Though I don't think she'll be able to take her GCSEs. Not in the short term. She's missed too much schooling. But that doesn't mean it wouldn't be valuable, I agree. So we could certainly look at some alternative education packages for her.'

'That sounds brilliant,' I enthused. 'It's really just what she needs, and as for the commitment bit, just leave that to me. How soon do you think you could get her in somewhere?'

Maggie laughed. 'You do sound keen! Soon, perhaps. It wouldn't be a regular school, but there is a unit I know of, quite local to you, actually, and I know they usually have a couple of places up for grabs. Tell you what, let me go and make a phone call or two. I'll get back to you in a bit. That sound okay?'

It sounded perfect, and the more I thought about it, the more keen I was to get it sorted, because it seemed to me that Emma's best shot at making a go of things with Roman would be rooted in her having that all-important independence from her ever less inspiring-sounding boyfriend. And the unit Maggie had in mind was one I already knew of. It was a place that took in ten or twelve teenagers at a time, kids who, for all sorts of reasons, had been excluded from mainstream school. Which didn't make it sound brilliant – that emotive word 'exclusion' covered many bases – but it wasn't just there to mop up the ne'er-do-wells. Kids came out of mainstream education for all sorts of reasons, and one of the common ones was because they had become teenage mums. And though it wasn't the ideal (that would have been going back to a regular comp and syllabus, obviously), it was definitely way better than nothing. I so wanted her to have a chance to spend at least a little more of her short childhood continuing her education and interacting with friends. It would stand her in such good stead in the long run and – most importantly – help to guide her towards making some better choices.

And to my surprise, Emma was very definitely up for it, even if not for the reasons I'd hoped.

'Result!' she whooped when Maggie called back a couple of days later with the news that, commencing the following Monday, she could attend the school for four days a week. I knew she was already upbeat because Tarim had finally deigned to text her, but her happy grin was really gratifying to see. 'Yes!' she said, punching a fist into the air, and scooping up Roman for a quick 360-degree spin-around. 'Now I get my laptop, don't I? Plus – woo hoo! Four days a week free of nappies and baby sick and free to be me again! Oh, thank you, thank you, Casey. Oh, let me hug you!'

I let her hug me – baby included – reflecting that even if her reasoning wasn't to be encouraged – particularly within earshot of Hannah – her enthusiasm definitely was. 'Hold up, though,' I said, as she released me and I took hold of Roman. 'Not so fast, missy. You'll be home at four, at which point you will be taking over full responsibility for your baby. Much as I love this little man, and I do –' I paused to tickle him – 'I will be very definitely handing him *back*.'

Emma nodded happily. 'Oh, course,' she said. 'Oh, you are such a star, Casey!' Then her brow furrowed. 'That's a thought. Is there a uniform?'

I shook my head, which had the effect of returning the grin to her pretty face. 'So I'll need clothes and that, won't I? So can we go shopping?'

'Perhaps,' I said, laughing at her newfound enthusiasm for education. 'I might be able to stretch to a couple of tops and a pair of jeans come Saturday, but right now you are a mum, dear, so here – can you grab Roman? Because I have to set about organising tea.' I laughed again as I watched Emma waltz off into the living room with the baby, and gave myself a mental pat on the back. At least I seemed to have cheered her up a bit.

'I think you're mad,' Mike had said when I finally fessed up to the plan I'd quietly hatched for us. And I knew he was probably right. The actual child-minding bit would be down to me completely; he'd be at work as per usual.

And it took all of seven days for me to realise he might be right. At the end of that first week – a week in which Emma had skipped off full of the joys of spring every morning, which was a complete turnaround – I was shattered, both physically and mentally. Despite my confident assertion otherwise to Riley, just a scant couple of months earlier, I had forgotten just how draining small babies could be. I lost count of the number of occasions, by the time the fourth day drew to a close, when I made a silent vow of solidarity with forty-something mothers. I was shattered. Not to mention mentally a bit numb. It didn't help that Roman was now becoming more demanding. Not only was he sleeping less and craving stimulation so much more; he was now really active in the daytime. And being almost five months old, he could now roll over on the carpet, so the days when he could be left in his chair playing with his feet were definitely over. He was also becoming inquisitive about the world around him and would get frustrated easily, so I was constantly having to find new ways to entertain him, in between feeding him and changing him, of course.

And my lovely home was suffering every bit as much as I was. It no longer looked much like the pristine place I took so much pride and joy in; it was beginning to resemble a very busy nursery, having been taken over by the triffid-like spread of baby paraphernalia. It was also killing me not to clean round Roman all day long, killing me. I could almost hear my marigolds crying out to me from the kitchen cupboard.

For Emma, however, school was manifestly a good thing. She was back engaging with the world – something she hadn't done in a long time; not without her child in tow, at any rate. And for that first week she was also sweetly grateful for what I was doing for her. Coming home and immediately taking over Roman responsibilities, she would talk animatedly about the school work she was doing and how much she was enjoying it, along with all the usual fourteen-year-old 'he said, she said' kind of gossip. It was good to hear, and I was really pleased for her; it was exactly what she should be doing, after all, and sitting at the kitchen table with her rabbiting on was just so nice, bringing back dearly cherished memories of when Riley and Kieron had been that age.

The meeting she'd had with CAMHS had gone well too. As I'd expected, but obviously couldn't take for granted, they weren't too worried about her, having decided that the incident had been a one-off, probably triggered by the stress of her unusual circumstances. Their feeling was that she didn't present a danger to herself or others, so they were happy to leave it at that. They were there, of course; the door was open if we had the slightest concern about her, or felt things were going downhill, but for now they were happy to sign her off.

Which was great news. But there was still a baby-shaped elephant present in the room whatever happened or didn't happen. And a Hannah-shaped elephant as well. And after a positive meeting with the latter on the Monday evening of the second week, everything did indeed begin sliding downhill. I didn't know if the two things were related – perhaps they weren't, perhaps it was just coincidence – but the day after Hannah's visit, and the pleasure of all those lovely positive noises she was making, Emma didn't get in from school till gone five-thirty.

'Where on earth have you been?' I asked her when she finally rolled up. 'Did you have something on after school that you forgot to tell me about or what?' Though I asked her the question, I knew very well that wouldn't have been the case. This wasn't a place that did after-school activities;

just getting through a normal school day would be challenging enough for some of the pupils there.

Emma treated me to the traditional fourteen-year-old eye-roll – not the best start to any attempt to appease me. But it seemed she wasn't about to try and make excuses for herself anyway. 'God, Casey, it's not *that* late,' she came back at me. 'I've just been hanging out with a couple of my friends. Can't you take a chill pill?'

'No,' I said. 'I can't. You have a baby here that needs feeding and playing with and bathing and changing, and I have a meal to prepare. Honestly,' I said, as she followed me into the kitchen, 'I'm disappointed, Emma. And after you impressed Hannah so much yesterday, as well.'

She rolled her eyes again and this time accompanied it with a heavy dramatic sigh. 'God, I knew you'd bring *her* up. I just knew it!'

It seemed to set the tone for the next few days. The following night – late again, even if not by quite the same margin – saw her scowling when I asked her to change Roman's nappy and then, when I impressed upon her that I'd had a busy and trying day, got back 'God, can't Casey-the-queen-of-the-carers cope?'

Which was the sort of backchat that would normally be water off a duck's back for me. Sure, I wouldn't stand for it, and with the kids on our specialist programme it would have resulted in an immediate loss of privileges, but it certainly wouldn't get to me, not from a petulant fourteen-year-old. But this time it did get to me – proof positive that the baby minding was exhausting me. 'Yes, the "queen of the carers" can cope perfectly well, thank you. No, young lady, I'll tell you what the matter is, shall I?' I railed at her. 'I don't appreciate you taking advantage of me, that's what. You have a phone, so if you're going to be late, then I'd appreciate it if you'd use it. I look after Roman so you can get yourself some education, not so you can come and go as you please!'

I could see Roman looking anxiously at the sudden commotion from his new high chair, and made a real effort to calm myself down. This was helping no one. Even Emma now looked shocked at my unexpected tirade. But perhaps that was no bad thing. That's what she'd lacked all her life. Boundaries. Good old-fashioned boundaries. 'Look,' I said more quietly. 'Would you please deal with Roman. I have things to do, tea to prepare, calls to make.' And seeing her assessing me and realising she might just have got away with it, I added, 'And don't think I'm going to put up with any more of this.'

Once they'd both gone upstairs and I'd got the kitchen straight I felt a little less frazzled. Though it occurred to me that perhaps we had only just begun to get to know the real Emma, that the traumatised, shy and vulnerable child-mother we'd taken in was only that as a result of her circumstances. In reality, this was a youngster who'd been at the receiving end of a very patchy and damaging child-hood and who, as a consequence, had probably become a very different animal – a girl used to having no one particu-larly mind, or care, what she got up to. Not until Tarim had come along, at least. It was ironic, I thought, as I beat

Mike's potatoes to a mushy pulp, that with Tarim in prison and my enthusiasm for getting Emma to reclaim some of her childhood, she was potentially going right back to what brought her to us in the first place, a girl who was used to being her own boss, answerable to no one – least of all a drink- and drugs-addicted mother. So having someone like me in her life, expecting her to toe the line, was a novel and unwelcome development. No wonder she balked at it. No wonder it caused friction. No doubt there would be further fun and games …

I would have that confirmed, as it turned out, only a scant couple of nights later, when she rolled up from school at 6 p.m. Worse than that, though, was that there was something new and unsavoury in the equation: the unmistakable smell of alcohol on her breath.

'Have you been drinking?' I asked her as she walked past me to get a glass of water. She didn't answer. She merely grinned and shook her head.

'I'm serious, Emma,' I told her, following her to the sink to study her better. She had a slight sheen of sweat about her and looked generally a bit off-colour. 'Have you had a drink?' I demanded. 'Truth now.'

'Oh, so what if I have,' she said. 'Don't I deserve one after all the shit I go through? Anyway, please don't start all this tonight. I'm *really* not in the mood.'

I was struck by her choice of words as much as her tone when she said them. Pound to a penny, I thought, her mother had said exactly that to her, and more than once. But now the tables had turned. And how appalling would it be if she jumped with both feet straight into her mother's shoes now. I had no choice but to give her both barrels. 'Emma,' I said levelly. 'How *dare* you speak to me like that. All I do is look after your baby all day long for you, and –'

She looked at me over the glass she was now drinking from, her eyes narrowed. Then she lowered it. 'I didn't ask you to do that, did I? You offered!'

'– and look after *you*,' I continued over her, 'from the minute you get home. Look after *both* of you. And I will not have you drinking while you're under my roof.'

'Well, it wasn't under your roof, was it?' she retorted. Then she laughed, but without mirth. 'And why you off on one anyway?' She was slurring, I could see it now. 'You get paid for doing it, don't you? 's not like you're doing it out of the goodness of your heart!'

I was that cross with Emma now that I needed something to fix on, so I went and plucked the baby from his high chair. My hands were shaking, I realised. And I could hardly bring myself to even look at her.

'Get upstairs and go to your bedroom,' I told her. 'You're obviously in no fit state to see to Roman. We'll talk about this tomorrow. Go on, hop it.'

She looked befuddled for a moment, but then her expression hardened, and she carried on drinking. And in that one instant I could see the depth of the damage in her innocent little girl's eyes. This was her territory. Drunken, vicious mother. Spiteful tongues. Casual cruelty. This was definitely her territory and I wanted no part in it.

'Go to your room, please,' I repeated, slowly and quietly.

She drained her glass. 'Suits me fine!' she barked at me, slamming it down on the draining board. 'You think he's your kid anyway! An' you better make the most of it, hadn't you? Because little d'you know that's all about to change. Yeah, *that's* right,' she said, as I cradled Roman's head against my neck. 'Cos his daddy's out any day now and he'll soon put a stop to all this "taking my fucking baby away" crap.'

And with that she practically staggered out, slammed the door, and lumbered heavily up the stairs, where hopefully she'd stay till she'd at least slept some of it off.

I stroked Roman's head absently as I stared at the kitchen door. Out of prison? If that were true then she was right. Things *would* be about to change. But there was something more pressing: how the *hell* didn't I know about it?

Chapter 10

Emma, that night, had been contrite. She came downstairs again, at around 8 p.m., puffy-eyed and pale, having presumably had a nap and (with the alcohol slowly wearing off now) a feeling of remorse beginning to wash over her. She apologised profusely, told me she wished she could take back all the nasty things she'd said to me, and then tearfully attended to Roman's needs for the rest of the evening and night. I didn't know if it was partly motivated by the report she knew I'd have to write for Hannah – which must have been on her mind – but when Saturday came, and Sunday, and she seemed to be making a real effort to make amends, I allowed myself to believe she really meant it.

But now it was the following Friday, and almost 7.30 in the evening, and once again she wasn't home from school. And as I jiggled a disconsolate Roman around on my shoulder and tried to do everything one handed, I reflected that the city of Rome wasn't built in a day any more than its tiny namesake.

I was disappointed, but I wasn't surprised by Emma's intermittent progress. In my line of work you would have to be extremely naïve to think that torn childhoods could be stitched back together quite that easily. It was mostly one step forwards then two – maybe even three – steps back with these children, till the happy day dawned when the numbers began reversing. And I was well aware that the one subject that Emma had skirted around most deftly since the previous week was that of Tarim. Yes, he was due out of prison fairly soon, she'd confirmed, but no, she didn't know quite when – he didn't either, apparently – she'd just said 'any day now' for effect. I had no choice but to accept that, whether I believed her or didn't. And my plan, given that I was next scheduled to speak with Maggie the following Wednesday, was to ask her what, if anything, she knew in that respect.

Rightly or wrongly, what I didn't want to do was act too hastily. Emma had spent most of her life, it seemed, being told by her mother that she was a piece of rubbish, so I knew that if I didn't accept both her apology and her assurance that I could, from now on, trust her, I would just be adding to the weight of worthlessness she already felt – a sure-fire recipe for reversing such progress as we'd already made.

But that required Emma not to abuse the trust I'd placed in her, didn't it? I glanced at the kitchen clock again and sighed heavily. And here she was doing just that.

'So, how long do you think we should give it before calling out the cavalry?' Mike asked, coming back into the kitchen with the last of the washing up. We'd gone ahead and eaten – Mike's job could be very physical, and he needed his dinner – and as he slid the last bits of crockery into the soapy water I put a plate over Emma's meal for when she did deign to roll in – though when she did, I mused, her tea would be the last thing on her mind, because I'd be filling it up with a large piece of mine.

'I don't know,' I said, as Mike took Roman from me. He was getting heavy now, and my back was really beginning to notice. 'There'll be no one in the office,' I said, 'and I'm really loath to call out the EDT only to have her waltz in here five minutes later. Quite apart from anything else it's not fair on them, is it? "Fourteen-year-old girl doesn't get home till eight in the evening" hardly constitutes an emergency, does it?'

'No, it's doesn't, to be fair,' Mike agreed. 'But you do have Maggie's mobile number. And, love, at some point soon you are going to have to call her. At the very least to see if she has any useful numbers – that friend, for instance; the one Emma was living with? She might be with her, mightn't she?'

I shook my head. 'They're not speaking,' I reminded him. 'Remember? Emma holds her responsible for putting her in this position in the first place. Well, she says she does. I'm not entirely convinced. Pound to a penny, she's actually just on Tarim's blacklist.'

I frowned as I said his name, and at the thought that came with it. 'D'you think that's it? That he's come out? D'you think that's where she is?'

Mike pulled a face at Roman, who tipped his head back and got a real case of the giggles. We were all he knew, and the thought struck me forcibly. Home for him was Emma, yes, but also Mike and me – we were his constants, his security, his significant others. And Kieron and Lauren, and Riley and David ... I pushed the thought away, because it was becoming an increasingly unpalatable one. That Roman knew nothing of the upheaval that he was soon to be at the centre of; that, whatever the circumstances – whether he stayed with Emma or got shipped off to another foster family – his routine, the voices he was used to hearing, the sights, the smells, the touch. Almost all of that would change, and change abruptly.

Mike was still gurning at Roman as he answered. 'I'd say if the answer to the first question's yes, then the answer to the second will be too.' He turned to face me. 'Don't you, love? You know I think it's time we gave Maggie a ring.'

And we would have done. Except that in the time it took me to finish the drying up, dig out the file, riffle through the papers to find Maggie's mobile number and punch the details into my phone contacts list, my own mobile buzzed into life in my hands. It was Emma's number.

It wasn't Emma on the end of the phone, however. It was a girl who introduced herself as Tash, one of Emma's new friends from the school, and who wondered if I would be able to go and 'fetch Ems home' from hers, as she was 'proper out of it, like', and she wasn't allowed to stay there because of the rules.

'Hey ho,' said Mike, as we jumped in the car and sped to the address we'd been given, having had Riley leap into action and take Roman for us, bless her. 'I didn't want to watch that episode of *Lewis* anyway.'

I laughed despite myself. After all, he'd recorded the whole series. He could watch it any time he liked, truth be known. But it was the sort of laugh that came when you were trying to do that whole anxious 'got to laugh or you'd cry' thing. And I *could* have wept. Not for me and not even for Emma. Just for the sheer frustration of having this whole thing playing out exactly as any cynic about 'Broken Britain' might expect it to.

As was the scene that greeted us when we got to the address we'd been given, which was what looked like a shared house on the edge of a big estate; the sort of supported set-up Emma herself might move to with Roman. The girl, who had a pretty round face and was dressed from head to toe in black, was apologetic, shy and also heavily pregnant, which would presumably account for her own sobriety. Which, in itself, made me warm to her immediately. She was obviously a girl with a sense of responsibility. She was also, understandably, a little wary, particularly when I asked her if Emma had been with her the whole time.

The answer to my question was no, apparently, though Tash was reluctant to be more specific. She would only tell us that Emma had been with her earlier, then gone off with some 'other friends', and that she'd come back with a plan to sober up before getting the bus home to ours, except – 'Well, as you can see,' Tash explained, with a world-weary air, 'it's not gonna be happening any time soon, is it?'

Indeed it wasn't. We went into Tash's small and impressively unscruffy living room to gather up her errant friend, and found her slumped on a little sofa, eyes shut. There was a plastic mixing bowl on her lap and a roll of toilet paper at her side, and I was glad to see that though much of the latter had been used up and scrunched around her, the former was empty, because if it hadn't been I'd have felt compelled to clean it up. Emma was properly drunk this time – properly out of it. And, though conscious and otherwise seeming okay (she had apparently stopped being sick now), she needed one thing above all others – to sleep it off.

'I'm sho shorry I'm wasted,' was all she could manage as we manhandled her into the car.

As at this time – and with her in this state – there really was no sense in trying to have a post-mortem with Emma, when we got her home we just made sure she drank a large glass of water, then I helped her undress and put her to bed. Mike, meanwhile, drove round to Riley's to pick up Roman, then, while I dealt with him, went up into the loft to get out the travel cot we'd bought for when the grandchildren were babies – there was no way we could let him sleep in with Emma tonight and it would be too much of an upheaval to try and manhandle his cot out of her room.

And, since Roman wasn't used to sleeping by himself yet, we took the view that a better night's sleep might be achieved if we just had him in our room with us.

'So what d'you think will happen now?' Mike wanted to know when we came back down. Little Roman, bless his heart, had gone out like a light, at least – he'd probably decided that the best refuge from all the commotion was sleep.

I rolled my eyes. 'What, you mean before or after I throw the frigging book at her?'

'I mean about this Tarim. I was talking to Riley about it – it's a point, isn't it? I mean, if he *is* sniffing around – and that was definitely the impression I got; that girl was very evasive, wasn't she? – then will they fix up regular contact, d'you think? Expect us to have him in the house? What? Because if he was with her tonight, and thought it was acceptable to leave her to get herself home in that state …'

He didn't need to say any more. I shook my head. 'I can't believe they'd do that, would they? I mean, she's denying he's the father specifically to protect him from social services. And that means he has no official rights in the matter. And as she's underage, what we say goes, pretty much, I'd say. So, no. I don't see why we'd have to have anything to do with him. I certainly hope not, in any case.'

I pulled out a kitchen chair and sat down on it. I felt shattered, both physically and mentally. Which was unlike me, as were the tears I felt prickling at the back of my eyes. I could cry for Britain, definitely, in all sorts of situations. I was as soft as they came when it came to kids, always had been. But the tears that threatened now were different; they were tears of sheer exhaustion – the result of taking on too much baby care as well as our errant teenager. The sort of tears that made the point that you were getting too strung up and should try to do something about it.

'But you know what really upsets me?' I said to Mike. 'That if he *is* out, and she *did* see him, that she couldn't just do that one thing. Just tell me, ask me, discuss it with me. Let me help her work something out, you know? After all those promises she made me. It's like it's all been thrown straight back at me. All of it. And when I really thought we were at last becoming close.'

Mike sat down beside me and put a strong arm around my shoulder. 'Hey, don't start,' he said softly. 'Don't you go off on one, beating yourself up, you hear? She's a teenager, plain and simple. And not just a normal teenager either, don't forget. Remember those things you always bang on about – boundaries? Of course you do. And she's had none of them, and she's hooked up with the first guy who's shown her any affection, by the sound of it, and had a baby, don't forget – all of which is a lot to deal with, by anyone's standards … love, even *you* are no match for all that.' He squeezed my shoulder.

'Yes, I know, but –' I began.

'And our job,' he continued, 'is simply to care for her and try to guide her – well, as best we can, anyway – till they decide what's going to happen to her next.'

'I know,' I said again, 'but if by "they" you mean social services and all these flipping assessment people, then we might as well hang up our gloves right now, because she seems determined to wreck it for herself, doesn't she? It's like she's on self-destruct autopilot. God, how have we so totally lost control?'

I was being a bit melodramatic, I knew, but even so this was a serious downward slide. I said so.

'No, it's not,' Mike said. 'This is just a blip. To be expected. It'll all seem a lot more manageable when we sit down and talk rationally about it tomorrow. I'm sure Emma will be mortified –'

'She was mortified last time ...'

'No, this time, *really* mortified. And we can sit down and see exactly where we are with this Tarim, and how best to go forward from here.'

He was right. Everything would seem so much more manageable in the morning. Except perhaps for Emma, who would no doubt have one hell of a hangover, though perhaps that in itself would help concentrate her mind. I checked the time. Not quite ten. Much too early for bed.

'Agreed,' I said. 'So, how about that *Lewis* after all? Nice relaxing murder. What d'you think?'

If I thought that was the worst that could happen, I was soon to be proved wrong. The following morning, just as Mike had predicted, Emma was once again full of remorse. I'd been up a good while by the time she surfaced (I'd forgotten just how many hours a teenager could sleep at a stretch), had fed, bathed and played with Roman, and by now put him back down for his morning nap.

I was in the middle of preparing her a bacon sandwich when she finally shuffled, dark-eyed and pale-faced, into the kitchen. I remembered teenage hangovers, even if not with Emma's evident regularity, and how something hot and greasy always seemed to do the trick.

The minute I smiled at her she burst into tears. 'Oh, Casey, I'm so sorry. I don't know why I did it, I really don't. I just … oh, God. If it helps any, I feel like utter crap.'

'It doesn't help, love, but I'll just tell you what my mum used to tell me – and that you'd do well to remember.' I waggled my fish slice in her direction. 'That you brought it on yourself.' I laughed then at the sight of her wan, miserable face as she gingerly pulled out a chair and lowered herself onto it. 'Come on,' I said, placing the plate in front of her. 'This'll help, I promise. As will this.' I popped a steaming mug of coffee down beside it. 'So do your best with it. Then you and I need to have a chat. Ideally before Roman wakes up again. So chop, chop.'

This made her blink back even more tears. 'I feel so bad that you had to have him all night, I really do,' she said, before taking a tentative nibble. Then she put the sandwich back down and pushed the plate away from her. 'Ugh,' she said. 'I don't think I can eat this. I feel really sick.'

'It'll pass,' I said, replacing the coffee with water. Perhaps it was still a bit too soon. 'Just take deep breaths,' I said. 'It'll settle. It usually does.'

She took the glass and sat back, drinking tiny sips while she watched me load the dishwasher. And when I'd done, I sat down across the table from her.

'Love,' I said. 'I know you feel terrible and I feel for you,
I really do. But right now I feel more terrible for that little
lad upstairs and that you doing this sort of thing means he's
not getting what he needs.' I looked hard at her. 'Tarim.
Did you see him last night?'

I probably couldn't have picked my moment any better,
as she was all out of energy or ideas with which to argue.
She simply nodded. 'He was there,' she said. 'Waiting for
me outside the unit when school finished. I hadn't planned
it or anything, Casey, honest. He just got out yesterday and
he came straight to see me. Before doing *anything* else.' She
paused to sip the water. I could see she was proud to have
been able to relate this evidence of Tarim's devotion. 'And
he does have a right, you know – I *am* his girlfriend.'

'Yes,' I said, trying to choose my words carefully. 'But
you have a phone, Emma, so why on earth didn't you use
it? If you had only rung me and explained that to me, then
we could have sorted something out.'

This seemed to spark something in her; something that
came from nowhere. Or somewhere, more accurately. The
very prison her beloved boyfriend had just come out of.
'Oh, right,' she said, 'like you'd have gone, "Okay Emma,
you just go off out and have a great time with Taz – don't
worry about the baby or anything." Yeah, sure!'

I got it then, in that instant, that perhaps she *had* wanted
to phone. I didn't know why – it was just a sense and I
trusted it. That she'd suggested to Tarim that she phone
me, even, but that he had told her not to – for the reasons
she'd just so pithily retorted.

So I bit my tongue. 'You know what I mean, Emma. Of course I wouldn't have said that; you're not stupid. You know that. But I would have understood that you wanted to see each other, and, as I say, we could perhaps have sorted something out. Could have arranged properly for me to look after Roman while you did see him. But instead you just *assumed* that I would look after Roman for you – you didn't even give me the choice – then went out drinking; the very thing you promised me you wouldn't do.'

'Of course I did – I had to! Taz has only just got out of prison, Casey – isn't it obvious that he'd want a drink?' She drew a stray few strands of hair from her forehead and looped them round her ear irritably. 'Anyway, you weren't always this old,' she reasoned. 'You'd have done stuff you shouldn't have when you were my age.'

I wanted to tell her that, yes, I had – I was only human, after all – but then I didn't have a baby when I was doing them, did I? But I knew it would fall on deaf ears. And I was much, much more interested in keeping her on side, where I could at least, hopefully, exert some small influence on what happened next, particularly now we had the added complication of Tarim to negotiate. 'Fair point,' I said. 'And yes, you're quite right. I had my moments. But this isn't about me – this is about you, and what's going to happen now. Are you planning on sneaking off with him every time you're out of my sight, or are you going to be responsible and sensible and remember that you're part way through an assessment with Roman, and that I need to report back to Hannah about your progress?'

The mention of Hannah's name seemed to trigger another strong reaction – breaking the illusion that this was a simple mother–daughter-style ticking off and that this particularly fourteen-year-old was in any way predictable.

'Oh, just do what you have to,' she said wearily. 'Grass me up if you want to.'

'Emma,' I said. 'The term "grass me up" isn't the right one. I am not here to "grass you up", as you put it. It's my job to help you do what you need to in order to show Hannah you're a responsible mum to Roman, and –'

'And you'll *still* be as bad as all those baby snatchers if you do grass me up. That's the problem,' she whined. 'No one will give me a fucking *chance*! Just like they never gave Taz a chance either! It's so stupid. If we were just left alone to get on with our lives there wouldn't even *be* this fucking problem!'

With her petulance came another loud-and-clear indication that she was a challenging teen – and still a young one – who needed those boundaries put in place right now. 'Emma,' I said sternly, 'I suggest you calm down. You won't like it, but you really need to take it on board, okay? There *is* a problem. You are fourteen and that *in itself* is a problem. Legally, it is a problem. However much you think your life would be better if we just left you alone, trust me, it wouldn't. And here are some facts. First of all you have been drinking underage – which is illegal. Secondly, the person who's been supplying you with alcohol has also been breaking the law as well. Now, if that's Tarim, then we have another problem right there, don't we? What with him just having come out of prison and all, that's not going to look very good for him, is it? Thirdly, like it or not, you are being scrutinised. You are being assessed to see if you can be a competent mother to Roman, and make no mistake, if things come out badly, then trust me, you will lose him. You will lose him because he has rights too, Emma. Don't forget that. You brought him into the world and he is your baby, no question. But we live in a civilised society only because there are laws in place to protect vulnerable people. And that includes Roman. He has a right to be taken care of properly and that's why he is protected by the courts. Do you get that?'

Since Emma had her head down and was listlessly prodding the bread of her uneaten sandwich with a finger, I had no way of knowing. But she had ears, and I knew she was listening.

'Finally,' I went on, just to press my point home, 'Mike and I have been very lenient with you up to now. You know that. And we've done this to give you *the best possible chance* of proving that you *can* look after Roman. But that only goes so far. You really have to shape up now. Roman deserves a good and caring mum, just the same as any child does. A mum, and possibly a dad, too, who will put *his* needs first. And if you're not going to do that, then I'm obliged to tell Hannah and Maggie. Do you understand what I'm saying, Emma? Do you?'

I had watched her throughout and I watched her still. She was now turning the glass of water around and around in front of her, using her palms. She finally stopped and looked at me. Perhaps the message had hit home. I was hoping for contrition; an acceptance, however sullen and grudging it might be, that it really was time to accept the seriousness of the situation – that if she didn't get her act together, she really *could* lose her baby.

But what I got instead took my breath away. 'Like I said,' she answered quietly, 'you go ahead and do you what you have to do. It's not in my hands, is it? It never has been, not since the minute I got pregnant. Social services always knew what they wanted. They wanted my baby so they could give it to some childless old couple somewhere. It's like Taz said, there's nothing we can do about it, is there?'

'Emma,' I said quietly, 'where is all this *coming* from? There is a lot you can do about it, trust me. *Everything* is in your hands.'

She shook her head. 'You really believe that? I don't. They're going to take him, Casey. Whatever I do. This whole thing is just them waiting till they've found their "perfect" family. And if they do take him, that's that, isn't it? We'll just have to wait till I'm sixteen, won't we?' She fixed her eyes on me, as if to see how I would react to her next words. 'And have another one,' she said. 'And then I'll be legal. So they won't be able to touch me then, *will* they?'

Emma stood up, then, picked up her glass and headed off back up the stairs, leaving me sitting there at the table, incredulous. I couldn't believe anyone could say what she just had and actually mean it. It was just down to her youth, I thought, her inability to cope, her background, her protective carapace, her hormones, her boyfriend. Oh, yes, her boyfriend – was that it? That he already had everything figured out? Be so much easier for him that way, after all. No mess. No baby with an underage girlfriend. No social services snooping around and sticking their noses in. Just dispense with this messy baby, wait a bit, and have another one. Excellent forward planning. God, I thought, distractedly. He was actually brainwashing her! Trying to get her to see the sense in letting social services deal with Roman. After all, this was a baby he had never even seen. Nothing more to him than an inconvenience, in all probability.

He, I decided, must be a *real* piece of work. But whatever the reasons, the facts remained the same. This was a potentially dangerous situation for Emma. I would have to phone both Maggie and Hannah and put them in the picture. The *full* picture this time.

Chapter 11

Back in my past life – before fostering, before I ran the unit in the local comprehensive – I worked for a time as an assistant team leader at a self-development programme run by the local council. Our job was all about taking young people who weren't in education, employment or training – commonly known as 'NEETs' – and helping them find a role in society. We would recruit groups of teens who had problems to overcome, and over the course of a full-time twelve-week period on the programme would help equip them with life skills, and nurture talents which would hopefully give them more confidence and ideally – the ultimate goal – a job.

There were two girls on one of these courses that I'd never forgotten. They were sixteen-year-old twins, called Scarlett and Jade, who'd been sexually abused for years by their father, not only individually, but also sometimes together; each being forced to watch as their sister was sexually assaulted. So theirs was the bleakest of bonds, and also a strong one, and since their mother had never stopped the unspeakable happening they had only each other to care about and care for. Their lives, though, since being in care, had taken very different turns. Scarlett had coped well, making progress and trying to get hers together while Jade, intellectually perhaps the brighter of the two, had gone the opposite way. She had fallen in with a bad crowd, taken to abusing drugs and alcohol and, perhaps inevitably, had fallen pregnant too. She'd been Emma's age when she had her first baby and it was taken away from her immediately. And then, very swiftly, she'd fallen pregnant again, and had another. That one was taken away from her too. It didn't bear thinking about. Her life was such a mess. And when I'd met her the effect on her was all too clear. She was back on the drugs, almost a recluse, and her self-esteem was so low that she looked and smelled on the outside every bit as grim and filthy as she undoubtedly, tragically, felt within.

Jade came through, though. In the end, we got her the help she so badly needed, and she was able, much to the relief of her distraught sister, to find a way out of the despair and grab at life again. But, by then, for her and her babies it was already too late. It was unlikely she'd ever see either of them again. I still thought about Jade often, and I thought about her now. I would sit Emma down, I decided, and tell her all about Jade. I didn't believe a word of what she'd said to me about just accepting she was going to lose Roman. And I so desperately didn't want that for her.

In the meantime it was Saturday lunchtime and I knew I had a weekend of uncertainty to face, because much as I knew I had to record and pass on the events of the past twenty-four hours, I wouldn't be able to discuss it with anyone now till Monday. I knew I could call John Fulshaw, but what would be the point, really? He'd tell us to use our judgement when it came to whether to allow Emma out of the house or otherwise, and my judgement already knew the answer to that one – that becoming her jailor probably wasn't it.

By now Emma was ensconced in the living room, watching telly. She looked markedly less green now but still very fragile, so it was just as well that Roman was so engrossed with the fun, squeaky toys attached to his play-mat, because I was determined not to step in and take over. Instead, I started getting lunch ready for when Mike came home from work, and pounced on him as soon as he walked through the door. He was expecting a quick bite to eat before going off to watch Kieron play football, but instead he got me trailing after him as he went upstairs to shower.

'Can you believe she said all those things to me?' I asked him. 'I was gobsmacked. To think that she could just write Roman off like that – and to say so to me! As if he was just a problem she and Tarim could do without – and that he could simply be replaced with another one.'

'She was saying it just to get a reaction out of you, I'm sure,' Mike soothed. 'Just like she did before – don't you think?'

'I know,' I said. 'I do know that. But it's really getting to me. It was the *way* she said it – it was like she and Tarim had already discussed it and decided that she was going to lose him, and didn't care.'

'Or more likely, I'd say, is that he's convinced her of that so well that she's steeling herself for it to happen – trying to act like she doesn't care. After all, after last night's shenanigans she's probably certain about that, don't you think? Probably just waiting for the knock on the door.'

'I know,' I said. 'But that doesn't *have* to happen. It's not a foregone conclusion. Not if we can make her see the seriousness of the situation; get her to take on board what needs to happen now. And him, though the more I hear of him the more I reckon pigs'll be winging their way past our bedroom window, frankly. But it *has* to happen. Because it seems to me he really does have to be a part of all this, jailbird and drug dealer or otherwise – because if they're already making plans for when she's "legal", as she put it, I don't see banning her from seeing him as an option, do you?'

'No, I don't,' Mike said, stripping off his shirt and throwing it on the bed. 'But right now I have a date with my own son and a football pitch and need a very big bacon and egg sandwich to fuel me up. Any danger of that happening any time soon, chef?'

But I was still on my track. 'But do you think we should do that anyway? You know, ban her just for the weekend, till we've had a chance to speak to Maggie? I thought not, but at the same time she *is* only fourteen still …'

'Love,' said Mike, 'you don't even need me to answer that. Long term or short term – makes no difference. If she chooses to bugger off with him every time he snaps his fingers, then we can't stop her. All we can do is point out that every time she does she's hammering a nail in her own coffin. Do what you've said you'll do – speak to Maggie and Hannah on Monday and tell them everything, and I mean everything. Why should we gloss over her slip-ups? She needs a reality check, love, and you're not doing her any favours by making out she's mum of the year when she so obviously isn't.'

'I hardly do that,' I bristled. 'I just want to give her the chance to prove she's adequate, that's all. Imagine losing your baby because of what's essentially just silly adolescent behaviour, and then realising what an idiot you'd been and wanting a second chance. Because there won't be one, will there? You know how these things happen. Once she's lost him …'

'I know, love. And I'm not trying to be horrible; just stating facts and consequences. And the fact is that this is in *her* hands, not yours. Though as far as this weekend is concerned what you can do is make it clear that if she wants to go out anywhere then she takes Roman with her – none of this gadding about while you babysit. You've agreed to childmind him while she goes to school, out of the goodness of your heart, but that's where it must stop. Now, are you going to feed me or what?'

* * *

134

I went downstairs again to make my poor starving husband some lunch, seeing his logic but with my heart fighting against it. Glancing into the living room, I could see Roman trying to attract Emma's attention and resisted the urge to scoop him up and pop him in his high chair in the kitchen so he could play with some bricks while I made Mike's sandwich.

As a mother myself I couldn't bear to think about a chain of events happening from which there would be no going back. And a chain which had an end point of a baby going into care permanently and a young mother scarred, now, for life. Still, as a responsible foster carer, I knew Mike was right. I mustn't keep covering up for Emma; I had a responsibility to Roman too, and had to do the right thing even if it broke my heart to be a part of it.

Tarim remained the elephant in the room till Sunday; present in everyone's minds but on nobody's lips. But if I thought Emma's silence on the subject of her newly released boyfriend was because she'd decided to part ways with him, I'd had to have been a top of the range idiot. Which I wasn't, so when her mobile started chirruping while we were in the dining room just starting our Sunday roast, I could tell she'd been waiting to hear from him just by her body language.

'Can I get that?' she asked, half-rising from her seat even as she spoke. 'It might be Taz and I don't have enough credit to call him back.'

I was about to answer, but Mike beat me to it.

'Go on, then,' he said, nodding. 'But be quick, okay?'

She pushed her chair back and ran to the kitchen, where the phone was – she'd taken to keeping her charger plugged in in there now, all the better, presumably, not to miss it.

'Hiyah, babe!' I heard her say to him. 'Whassup?'

With the house being so open plan, we could both hear her clearly, so, while Roman played enthusiastically with his pureed bowl of roast dinner, Mike and I ate methodically and listened.

'I'll see what Casey says,' I heard her tell him. 'I know. Yeah, I *know*, but I still have to *ask* …' There was a pause then, which was followed by 'C'mon, don't be like that, babe. Okay, babe. Half an hour then. By the shops. Okay, love youuu.' Then silence. She returned.

'You planning on going out, then?' Mike asked as she sat back at the table. Roman was by now splatting his spoon into the mush in the bowl in front of him. I was pleased to see Emma automatically reach out and take the spoon from him, and then encourage him to eat with it as well as play with it.

In her own food, however, she suddenly seemed to have little interest, pushing it around on her plate.

'Erm, well, yes,' she said. 'That was Taz.'

'We guessed that,' I said mildly, smiling.

'And he wondered if I could take Roman out for a walk, you know, to see him. Just for a walk for a bit, like. Just down to the shops and stuff.'

This floored me. I'd been expecting to have a completely different problem – that of pointing out that we were not prepared to babysit while she went to meet Tarim, that, following on from the conversation we'd already had on Saturday, further arrangements regarding him must be sorted out with Maggie.

So I was thrown. And since Mike and I couldn't go off and have a summit talk, I did my thinking about what to do on the hoof, solo.

'Take Roman *with* you?' I said. 'Love, we can't let you do that, I'm sorry. You know we're not able to allow contact till Maggie agrees it. But look, if you want to go out for an hour –'

'Why?' she wanted to know. 'He's my baby, not yours. Tarim just wants to *see* him. There's nothing wrong with that!'

Mike gave me a warning glance, which was understandable. Hadn't we already agreed there'd be no babysitting till things were sorted out? 'Casey's right,' he said to Emma. 'We haven't been cleared to allow Roman contact with Tarim, so until we've spoken to Maggie and Hannah in the morning I'm afraid that can't happen. Love,' he said gently, 'you've got to realise that you're in care and we're in a position of responsibility for both you and Roman, and that includes keeping him away from people who've just been released from jail. Like I say, if the authorities say different, then it'll be fine, but in the meantime ...'

Emma rounded on Mike then, looking daggers at him. 'Oh my *God*!' she said, her voice rising. 'You people make me sick. I could have lied to you right then. Easy. I could have just said I was taking him out for a walk or something, couldn't I? Or meeting up with Tash. I could've said it was Tash, couldn't I? And you wouldn't have known any different! But, no, I decided to be honest and where does that get me? Nowhere. Great! Thanks for that!'

She scraped her chair back again, threw her fork across the table and stomped out of the room, slamming the door for good measure.

There was a moment of silence, Roman blinking in shock at the place where his mother had just been. He put his little spoon down and held both arms out towards me, wanting a cuddle. I went across and scooped him up, almost on autopilot.

'She has a point, love,' I said to Mike as I sat back down again with Roman on my lap. 'She could have lied. Easily. She's right – we wouldn't have known.'

'Casey, have you heard yourself? We just heard the bloody conversation, didn't we? How could she have denied it? We were three feet away! I hope she doesn't think we're that stupid!' He put his own cutlery down and retrieved the errant fork from the floor beside his chair. 'Don't be falling soft, love,' he went on, 'for God's sake. She isn't old enough or mature enough to be making those kinds of decisions. Leave her to stomp all she wants. He stays here and that's that.'

And that *was* that. We heard the front door slam a few minutes later, signalling that Emma had gone out to meet Tarim by herself. And by the time she returned – a full two hours later – I had already bathed and dressed Roman in his night clothes and we were settling down to watch a movie on TV.

Emma purposely breathed out in my direction as she leaned down to take Roman from me. 'See,' she said as I blinked at the sudden gust of air in my face. 'No alcohol – just in case you were wondering.' Upon which she flounced out, throwing a 'Don't worry, I'm taking him up to chill with *me* now' back at me as she did so.

I got up early the next morning; saw the dawn in fully dressed, in fact. And after Mike had gone to work, and with both Emma and – surprisingly – Roman still sleeping, retrieved and updated all the notes I kept in my desk drawer.

Keeping detailed notes is part and parcel of the business of fostering. It was important to log everything that happened. This was both to provide a comprehensive record of a child's progress – or lack of – and, equally importantly, to protect a foster family against allegations. Which did happen – when a child or teenager became a member of a foster household, much that went on obviously did so behind closed doors. And with many children in care being there because of things that had happened behind other closed doors, it wasn't surprising – even if it was depressing – that a foster carer could be the victim of false allegations.

Day-to-day events were recorded in a log book which had to be kept for at least a year after a child left the placement, just in case such a thing did ever happen. And if there was an incident that could potentially have serious ramifications immediately, e.g. an episode of aggression, threat or actual violence, then the procedure was for me to call the emergency duty team and take further advice from them.

I had a thorough read-through of my notes and, as I did so, I began compiling a short list of the questions I'd need to ask Maggie and Hannah. My plan was to call John Fulshaw first, just to update him on the situation, then call Maggie and, last of all, Hannah. It wasn't a task I was looking forward to, especially that last one, but an hour, three strong coffees and several thoughts of lambs and slaughter later, I finally picked up the phone.

Chapter 12

Contact was denied. Which was no surprise to me whatsoever. When a child is in care, social services have the ultimate sanction and must act in that child's best interest at all times. This meant they were more rigorous than many parents might be in the same circumstances; if Tarim wanted to see Roman, he had to jump through several hoops, all of them put there with that in mind. He would need to be assessed by a separate social worker in order to ascertain his suitability to be around children generally; to provide evidence that he was a responsible adult. He wouldn't be assessed in the same way as Emma – she had to be seen to be capable of caring day to day for her baby – but it would still involve seeing Tarim and interviewing him in either his own home or that of his parents.

There was also the business of him having come out of prison without anyone key in social services having known about it. He would have been allocated a probation officer

and, as far as I remembered from the notes I'd had originally, there should have been communication between
whoever that was and the office Maggie and Hannah
worked from about when that day was happening so we
could all be prepared.

And we should have been. And would have been, except
that the information was passed to Maggie on the day she'd
gone off for a few days' leave. Not that it made any difference now. What had happened had happened. The main
thing now was to factor the nineteen-year-old in to the
equation and plan a strategy that, of necessity, included him.

I still knew little about Tarim, but I did know that though
he had been given his own flat he'd spent most of his time
since he came out staying with his father. Not that it made
a great deal of difference where he lived, as I didn't have
either address. No, if she were serious about it happening,
that would need to come from Emma. But in the meantime, no Tarim. And I had to tell her.

When Emma finally surfaced I could tell she was still
brooding about the events of the previous day, and that –
news or no news delivered about the Tarim situation – we
were in for a less than jolly day.

'Oh, right!' she said, slamming the fridge door shut in
disgust, having ascertained that there were no bottles
prepared for her. I'd normally do them, being first up, but,
with my batch of phone calls to deal with, today I hadn't.
'So this is how it's gonna be from now on, is it?' she huffed.
'Take it out on the baby, why don't you?'

She plonked Roman down on the cold tiled floor and set about banging empty bottles around on the worktop.

'Emma,' I snapped, exasperated, 'do you really think I'd be so petty? I've been busy. Besides, it's not my job to make bottles up for Roman anyway, is it?'

She ignored this and scowled as she slapped the switch on the kettle. It immediately flicked off again, the kettle being empty. 'Well, you seem to be,' she snapped straight back, plucking the kettle from its stand and taking it across to jam under the cold tap. 'I thought you were on my side, not theirs!'

I just about stopped myself from asking her to lift the lid up and a fountain of water sprayed all over the floor. She cursed. 'But you're just like the rest of them,' she went on. 'Trying to make my life as difficult as you can!'

Stepping around Roman, I went to get my dusting things out of the cleaning cupboard. There was no point in even engaging with her while she was in this kind of mood, much less spelling out the Tarim situation. I also had to chase away the thought that maybe I'd miscalculated in being so keen on this placement. It seemed the worst of both worlds: a teenage girl with enough attitude to head-line at Glastonbury Festival and a dear little baby I had to steel myself to lose. How simple, it suddenly seemed, to have, say, a routinely challenging eight- or nine-year-old, and I looked back at previous placements – dear little Jenson, sweet little Georgie, cheeky Spencer – with glasses so ridiculously rose-tinted that they could have had a walk-on part in a Barbara Cartland novel.

I mentally shook myself. Ridiculous was about right. With hardly an exception every single child Mike and I had fostered had gone through periods every bit as grim and challenging. I was just tired, weighed down by the news (and its potential consequences) that I was all too soon going to have to impart. I gathered up my cleaning things. Tonight, that would be best. I'd save the Tarim discussion till then, I decided. When Mike was home and there to support me. Just for today, I'd had enough confrontation.

Even so, it still hurt that Emma could turn on me like this. It wasn't about sides – that was silly – but if it had been, the same applied. I was on hers. I was rooting for her. I only wanted the best for her. And though I knew most of her ranting was down to tiredness and hormones it still felt like a slap to be treated like this. I felt relieved when, armed with a baby bottle and some porridge, she huffed back upstairs to her room.

But by the time Riley came over for a sandwich at lunchtime, I was struck by an unfamiliar and unwelcome new feeling. A kind of empty feeling – not the sort that would be accompanied by massed violins, exactly – just this sense that things weren't quite okay.

'Simple,' said Riley. 'It's that feeling you always described as an "empty nest thing".'

That made no sense. 'How could it be that?' I asked her. 'You get that when you haven't got any kids left. I'm flipping surrounded by them right now, it feels like.'

'No, it is that, Mum, honest. I never really got what it meant when you said that but since I've had the boys I do get it. I feel like that, like, when David's mum takes the boys out for the day or something. Just this slightly lost feeling, like something's missing but I don't quite know what. Bet it's that.'

'But why would I be feeling that?' I persisted.

'Durr, mum,' she said, grinning at me. 'Haven't you noticed? You've been looking after Roman pretty solidly for something like six months now, haven't you? Then, suddenly, the past couple of days, she's been keeping him from you …'

'Well, not quite keeping him from me. It's not like that, exactly …'

'Yes, it is. And what difference does it make anyway? You're used to being with him all the time. Okay, so not 24/7 but most of his waking hours – and a lot of yours. Plus you've been looking after him while Emma's been at school, too, don't forget. It *is* that, Mum – pound to a penny. Empty nest.'

Who knew my daughter could be so insightful? She was probably right, too. In fact, the more I thought about it, the more it made sense. Emma wasn't suddenly becoming mum of the year, admittedly, but she was trying to let me know who was in charge here; that it was her who controlled how much time I spent with her son. It was a slightly uncomfortable feeling.

'You're right, love,' I said to Riley. 'I'm my own worst enemy, aren't I? Always way too ready to jump in, Mrs Indispensible, doing everything. And just making it more difficult for me to let go. Though there's no doubt I should.

For both their sakes. And for mine, come to that. I'm getting fed up of doing it all anyway, truth be told.'

Riley laughed. Loudly. 'Mother,' she said, 'you know as well as I do that you'll do no such thing. You're just peeved that someone else is taking control, for once. But you should – you should leave her to it. That way she'll soon come to realise just how much you *have* been doing for her. She needs you – she'll soon come to recognise that. Just take a break while you have the chance – tell you what, let's go shopping tomorrow, shall we? Leave her to it for a change. Do her good.'

I felt much better after Riley went, and a good deal more relaxed. And with Emma spending much of the rest of the afternoon up in her room with Roman, I enjoyed preparing a huge home-made lasagne for our tea. Nothing better on a cold, early March evening than a carb-laden plate of pasta. Not that, when it came to it, the atmosphere smelled quite as good as the food did. Roman was napping, and without the focus of having to entertain and feed him the mood round the table was sombre. It was sad; Emma had been with us for almost half a year now, but it was as if we were a trio of strangers. Even Mike, usually so good at making light, banterish conversation, had given up and had his gaze firmly on his dinner.

It was Emma, in fact, who spoke first. 'So,' she said, out of the blue, 'any news from the baby snatchers? What's the verdict? Can Tarim start seeing Roman or not?'

'Not. That's the short answer,' Mike replied, equally testily. 'At least not just yet,' he added, his tone softening slightly. Then he looked at her again. 'And before you start jumping down anyone's throat,' he said, 'just listen to what Casey has to say first.'

Ah. Over to me, then. I duly jumped to attention. 'Right,' I said. 'Well … first of all, they accept that you'll want to see Tarim – if that's what you want to do, that is. Though, I have to tell you, they don't like it. I might as well be honest, Emma; the truth is that Maggie's told me that they feel he's a bad influence on you.'

'They know hardly anything about him!' Emma snapped.

I refrained from pointing out that they didn't really need to, given that what they did know comprised 'prison' and 'drugs'.

'They're just a bunch of arseholes who won't give him a chance,' she then told us. 'And too right I can see him – I'll do what I want! And that includes Roman seeing him, whether they like it or not!'

'Well, actually no, Emma,' I told her calmly. 'You won't be doing that. If Tarim wants to be part of Roman's life he has to be assessed first, just as would anyone else who wanted to play a part in his upbringing. After that, then they will decide if he's an appropriate person to have contact. And he might also be expected to go on a parent-ing course, just like you did when you were pregnant. I know you don't like it, love,' I finished, 'but it's a serious business agreeing to contact, and that's what they've decided, so I'm afraid that's it for now.'

She leapt to her feet then, knocking her chair over, and I got the impression she'd been expecting this all day. After all, she might be headstrong but she wasn't stupid. 'Well, fuck that!' she screamed. 'And fuck the two of you as well! I'm not staying in this fucking house a single minute longer!'

Mike had stood up as well now, and he righted her chair. Upstairs, I could hear that Roman had begun bleating too. Emma turned to Mike. 'Oh, don't worry,' she spat. 'I'll be leaving your precious baby. Just for tonight. So make the most of it, okay!'

I breathed deeply. Only a fourteen-year-old could tell you to f*** off out of their life while at the same time pointing out you'd also be in charge of babysitting duties. Seen like that, it was even slightly amusing.

But not from where Emma stood, clearly. 'You can stay right where you are,' Mike snapped at her, as she headed for the hallway. He raised his voice just enough to ram his authority home. 'We haven't finished discussing this yet and you are only fourteen years old, young lady. You can't just up and off every time things don't go your way. How will you cope living alone with Roman when things go wrong, eh? Just run away then too, will you?'

'Oh piss off, Mike,' she said. 'I'm off and you can't stop me. And don't bother looking for me because Taz'll come and pick me up in his car.' She grabbed her phone then, and I heard the swish of her raincoat being swept from the banister. 'I'll be back for Roman tomorrow,' she shouted back, as if her baby was no more going to keep her there than if he'd been her hamster. 'And by the way,' she added, as she yanked on the door handle, 'I'm nearly fifteen, if you don't mind!'

And with a slam of the front door – her speciality – she was gone.

I felt sick to my stomach, and wished I hadn't already eaten most of my lasagne. I slid the plate away crossly. 'Now what?'

Mike scowled. 'Don't blame me, love!' he said. 'You heard her! I know what's happened here – she's already arranged to go and meet the little … hmm, yeah, that's what's definitely happened. Of *course*. She was angling for that row just to give her the excuse to get out of here.'

'I'm not blaming you,' I retorted. 'But we can't just leave it, can we?'

'What, the rest of our dinner?' He sighed heavily and rasped a hand across his chin. 'For the moment we can,' he said. 'For the moment. Yes, I think we should just leave it.' He nodded towards the ceiling. 'You going up for that little man up there or am I?'

We agreed that we would give Emma a couple of hours to cool off. It was still only six – not even dark yet – and if we phoned the emergency duty team at this point we'd just look like idiots. But I didn't want to just leave it so I called Maggie on her mobile to ask her advice. She felt the same. No point in causing even more of a drama. 'Leave it a bit longer,' she counselled. 'I don't doubt she'll come back of her own accord before too long, but, if she doesn't, call her mobile, and only if she doesn't answer would I go to the next step.'

In the end, we gave it till 8.30 before trying to get hold of her, and when we did she didn't answer her mobile. That was it for me. 'Mike,' I said,' I want to ring EDT now. And the police –'

'Steady on –' he began.

'No, I'm going to,' I told him. 'I just have this feeling and I really don't like it, Mike.'

He got up from where he'd been sitting, half watching the television, and switched it off with the remote.

'I know you and your feelings, love, but I have one idea I think we should try first.' He pulled the blind up and peered out, then put it down again. 'You wrap the baby up nice and warm and let's drive to that girl's house. Tash, was it?' I nodded. 'Let's go and see if she can help us. She might have gone there again, mightn't she? And even if she hasn't, she might be able to throw some light on where she is. What do you think?'

I thought it was a brilliant idea. Despite knowing I must, I was still reluctant to call out the emergency duty team – it would take things to a whole other level to do that, and perhaps to a point where things couldn't be undone. It would be in black and white on Emma's record: immature and irresponsible. I flew upstairs to wake and dress Roman, remembering to grab his teething gel as I went.

* * *

We drove slowly round the estate we'd come to on our previous excursion, Mike up front, looking like a cabbie, and me in the back seat, nursing Roman. He was grizzly now, both from being woken and from the teething, and for a moment or two I regretted our impetuosity in bringing him out. Perhaps the better thing would have been for just one of us to have come out looking, but as we'd already decided, Mike alone might not be able to persuade Emma to come back with him, and there was no way he'd have let me go instead.

We passed numerous groups of teenagers, who all eyed us in different ways, some incuriously, some suspiciously, some openly stopping to look and scrutinise. It wasn't a nice place to be with a baby at approaching ten at night.

Mike was more bullish than me, and twice, when we saw groups that seemed to be of girls around Emma's age, wound down his window to ask them if they knew of or had seen her. I wasn't surprised to note that both groups seemed to know of both her and Tarim, but if they knew where either of them was they weren't saying.

Eventually we found our way back to the house we'd collected Emma from the previous time, and I stayed in the car with the baby while Mike went to the door. It was a forlorn-looking place; the external plaster chipped and stained, the tiny strip of front 'garden' no more than a scrubby and neglected place to keep the various recycling bins.

But when Tash came to the door I remembered the neat, cosy interior and was reminded that what you saw on the outside of these places didn't necessarily reflect what was going on inside.

Mike chatted with Tash for a minute or so, then someone else appeared at the door. It seemed to be an older woman – one of the staff whose job it was to keep an eye on the teenage mums there, probably, or an older relative – and I could tell from her arm movements that she was now directing Mike somewhere else.

He was back soon after, rubbing his hands together before gripping the wheel and starting the engine. 'Brrr, it's cold out there,' he said. 'You know, you'd never think that was a kind of hostel, would you? Be great if Emma can go to a place like that, wouldn't it? Anyway,' he continued, turning the ignition key, 'I bring good news. I have an address.'

'Thank God for that,' I said. 'She's seen Emma tonight then, has she?'

'Apparently not actually seen her. But it does seem that they've texted. That was the on-call social worker I was talking to, by the way,' he added. 'Thank goodness she was there still. Don't know if I would have got it out of Tash otherwise. She's obviously fiercely loyal to Emma –'

'Which is a good thing, on balance.'

'Exactly. Though if I was being less charitable I might be tempted to think it's more to do with her being scared of Tarim, don't you think?'

God, this boy – no, grown man – was really getting to me. I wasn't exactly looking forward to meeting him exactly, but I was certainly keen to, just to put a face to his already extremely tarnished name.

We pulled out into the main road that ran through the estate again. 'It's going to be a bit of a doss house, by all accounts,' Mike warned, looking at me via the rear-view mirror. 'Bit of a meeting place, apparently – when lots of the local kids go to chill. And drink. And smoke dope. And other unsavoury things, no doubt. Sounds like our Tarim's a real party planner, eh?'

'Lovely,' I said, glancing at his son.

Mike painted a pretty unappetising picture, but it paled into insignificance compared to the sight that greeted us round the next corner. We had arrived, it seemed, but not to a doss *house* – not in the bricks and mortar sense. It was actually a group of four high-rise flats, their tops reaching dizzyingly high in the night sky, most of them liberally peppered with smashed windows, no windows or boarded-up windows and graffiti liberally sprayed on most of the vertical surfaces. Around them all lay a large expanse of weedy, fractured concrete, and the whole thing was finished off with a community of various wheelie bins, accessorised by split and spewing rubbish bags.

Mike leaned forward in his seat, the better to peer upwards and take in the view.

'I think you'd better come with me, love,' he said, 'and bring the baby, too. It's up on the third floor and I'm not happy about leaving you both down here.'

Roman had just dropped off to sleep and I was loath to disturb him. 'Go on, love, I'll be fine,' I told him. 'In fact,' I said, opening the rear door, 'I'll pop into the front. Leave the engine running and I'll have the radio on. I'll be fine.'

He looked around. 'I don't know, love …'

'Mike, there's nobody around. I'll be fine.'

'Nobody you can see,' he corrected. 'This looks like the sort of place where there could be all sorts, all lurking in the shadows.'

'Mike, will you just get up there, please?' I said, transferring to the front passenger seat. 'I'll lock myself in, and if anyone comes out and starts looking suspicious I'll put my hand on the horn and leave it there, okay?'

So Mike did, albeit reluctantly, and as I watched him go through the splintered front door I shuddered. I didn't feel quite so brave now he'd disappeared from view. I ticked myself off, telling myself not to be ridiculous – out loud, too. I'd seen worse, been to worse places, dealt with some pretty frightening scenarios. There was nothing to scare me here but fear itself. Heebie jeebies. Still, I was glad, as the minutes ticked slowly by, that I didn't actually see or hear anyone.

In fact, the next person I did see was Mike once again, coming through the doors fifteen minutes later, to my great relief. I'd been through a process – when he hadn't come out straight away I'd been worried, and then, as the time passed, was reassured by his continued absence – she must obviously be there – and then, as more time went on, began imagining different scenarios. She wasn't there at all. He'd been mugged, he'd been beaten up, perhaps drugged … I was just giving myself another stern talking to when he appeared – and more importantly, appeared fit and well.

It was a second or two later when I realised he wasn't alone either – that the dim light in the hallway was silhou-etting two other people, and as they emerged I realised one of them was Emma.

The other was a male and, as they become more visible, I realised I was finally seeing Tarim.

They lingered in the doorway, while Mike jogged back to the car. I wound the window down. 'What took you so long?' I said. 'And what's going on now?'

'Sorry, love,' he answered. 'Just been in summit talks, that's all. I've had a good talk to both of them and I think they're seeing reason.' He grinned then. 'No houseful of down-and-outs – just the two of them, looking sheepish. Emma's quite upset, to be honest. I think she's really torn.' He squatted by the car door. 'Trying to do what's best – you know? Torn between doing the right thing and also keep-ing me laddo here happy …'

'So is she coming with us now?' I asked, looking past him to where they waited.

Mike nodded. 'Yes, she is. With one provision. He wants to see our little man here. Just for a minute or two, and, honestly, love, the lad looks genuine. I said I'd ask you. Check you were happy. See what you said.'

I was shocked, and I'm sure my expression showed it. Mike was the one who'd been the most adamant about no contact, so this was a turnaround. But should we? How did we know he wouldn't snatch Roman and run off with him? I didn't think he would – this was the boy who'd pointed out how easily they could replace him with a new model, after all – but, even so, contact was contact and was denied for a reason. This was a convicted drug dealer, and though that was the offence that sent him to prison, in my experience there were usually other offences involved as well. We had to be responsible.

I glanced across and could see the pair of them, watching me intently. And tried to rationalise. What could happen, really? Mike was here, and a good head taller than Emma's errant boyfriend. Not to mention wider …

'Okay,' I said, 'just for a couple of minutes. If that's what it's going to take, then so be it. But I'm going to have to record it – or the pair of us'll be the ones that find themselves in trouble. Tell them to come over here, though. It's too cold to be walking about with him.'

Mike's smile was broad. 'I'll go and tell them. Two minutes and that's that. Then at least they can't accuse us of not being understanding, can they?'

He whistled across to them and beckoned them to join us at the car while I got out, unbuckled Roman's car seat and lifted it out. I put it gently on the bonnet of the car. The pavement just seemed way too grim a place for it.

Emma was there first. 'Thanks so much, Casey,' she said in a small voice. She looked wan in the evening gloom, and, without make-up, not a day more than her age. In fact, younger.

I turned to Tarim, who shocked me – also. He was a good-looking lad, dressed in the standard uniform of his age and type – the sort of jeans that started halfway down his buttocks and puddled above his pristine trainers, and a tatty-looking leather jacket that could have either been naturally or artificially distressed. But it was his youth that struck me most – he just looked so ridiculously young. In my head I had this vision of a hardened, swarthy criminal, but, of course, he wasn't so old himself. The age of eighteen might well mark the start of a man's adulthood, but this lad – and he was a lad – was all bum fluff and dewy skin. He was slight, too. I tried to imagine him in the harsh, uncompromising setting of a male adult prison, and I couldn't. I just couldn't, at all.

'Here,' I said, proffering the car-seat handle. 'Take him for a minute. He might be grumpy, mind – he's teething. Not to mention very tired.'

Emma had the grace to look guilty, as she watched her boyfriend set the car seat down on the pavement, very gently, then squat down and look intently at his son.

'Hello, baby boy,' he said, grinning. 'How you doing?' His teeth were bright white against his olive skin.

To my complete surprise, Roman grinned right back at him.

'I'm sorry, mate,' Tarim said quietly, making me feel almost embarrassed to be intruding. 'I'm sorry I haven't been there. I really, really wish I could've. But I will be. I will be now, mate. We'll make it work.'

If it had been scripted for a movie, it couldn't have moved me more. I felt a lump grow in my throat and glanced at Mike, who seemed to feel the same. What shocked me most was that I didn't expect to feel this way at all. I expected to feel angry on Emma's behalf, judgemental about Tarim – even though that wasn't normally like me. I expected to feel nothing but negative about this stupid boy who'd contributed to messing up all their lives.

But I didn't, and when Tarim stood and said, 'Oh, Ems, he's beautiful. He's just beautiful,' all thoughts of telling him what a crappy boyfriend he'd been, and how he should leave them both alone and get the hell out of their lives, disappeared in a flash. Instead I felt moved, and very heavy of heart. Because all I could think was what a shame this all was and just how slim were the chances of them ever making it work. Because that was the problem with real life, wasn't it? That it just wasn't scripted like a movie.

Chapter 13

Sleep didn't come easily that night. I just couldn't seem to shift the image of Tarim looking down so tenderly at his baby. It just didn't fit, that was the problem. Didn't fit with my pre-formed image of a teenage ne'er-do-well and jailbird, and I was struggling to reconcile the two.

Emma had cried as we left Tarim, and cried on the journey home. But it had been a different kind of crying; it was soft, quiet, defeated. As if in that one tender exchange between her baby and his father she'd seen the same things as I had – that it was all hopeless, that it shouldn't have worked out like this.

I tried to feel hopeful as I chewed everything over, sleep eluding me. Perhaps there *was* hope now for a happy ending. Nothing was settled yet, after all. But there was this feeling gnawing at me, from deep in the pit of my stomach, a heavy sense that it was probably all too little too late. Much as I hated to confront the idea, the fact was that, behind the scenes, maybe Emma was right – that plans were already being made to remove Roman from her care. I really hoped not, and tossed and turned, trying to fathom a way to stop that happening. Not an easy task. That was my last thought before I eventually fell asleep.

I felt no less gloomy the next morning. I stared out of the kitchen window, barely registering the prettiness of the garden or the bright, penetrating sunshine, focusing only on the spoon stirring my coffee as I waited for the rest of the house to wake up. It wasn't very often that I got up before Mike, so I decided to treat him – popping eggs in a pan and bread in the toaster, so I could prepare his breakfast before his alarm went off. And as I looked out again, I saw a couple of late miniature daffodils poking out from the dingy under-growth beneath my rose bushes. There was a metaphor right there, I thought, in those robust little flowers. A hope-ful metaphor for what might transpire later. Something nice coming out of what on the surface looks dark. Well, I decided, there was no harm in hoping, was there?

Mike was predictably stunned and delighted by his surprise of boiled eggs and soldiers, and his happy mood as he left for work gave me another welcome injection of positivity. No, I wasn't about to be economical with the truth when I made the phone calls that needed making, but neither was I going to pre-judge what the outcome might be.

'Morning, love, morning, baby!' I said brightly, tickling Roman under the chin, as he and Emma came down and joined me at around nine. 'There's some fresh toast and jam there,' I went on, 'and some coffee in the jug, too. Oh, and Roman's bottle's warmed, if you want to settle him with it before you eat.'

Emma looked wan – like she'd had even less sleep than I had – and I felt sorry for her. She wasn't due in to her unit till lunchtime today, which was a blessing. 'Love,' I said, 'I've got to phone Maggie Cunliffe now, like I told you. You know I have to do that, don't you?' Emma nodded as she transferred Roman to her other hip. 'It's the only way,' I said. 'The only way we're going to straighten all this mess up. And don't worry – I haven't forgotten this is your lives we're talking about, not just Roman's. So I'll be telling her about your and Tarim's wishes, too.'

She nodded again, looking tearful, and I put a hand on her arm. 'It'll be okay, love,' I said. 'Let's just see what they have to say, eh?'

'Yeah,' she said. Just 'yeah'. No 'whatever'.

I went out and sat in the garden to call Maggie. Perhaps the proximity to those unexpected blooms would bring good luck. Not that I should see Maggie as an adversary, because she wasn't, but having met Tarim now, and feeling so unexpectedly ambivalent about what should happen next for these two kids, I couldn't help but feel slightly gladiatorial.

'Oh dear,' said Maggie, once I'd outlined the events of the last few days and alerted her to the email already in her inbox. 'I hadn't realised things were heading in this direction, Casey. And I certainly didn't realise that Tarim had been making waves as far as Roman is concerned. And you say they've been seeing each other. Did you and Mike agree to this?'

I bristled at this. 'Hardly,' I said. 'It certainly wasn't on our agenda. Maggie, it's not been easy, this. If Emma goes out Mike and I don't follow her. We didn't know Tarim was out and about to *be* seen by Emma, did I? Anyway, the point is that we *have* made clear that he can't have contact till it's been authorised, but last night when we picked her up we both made the decision that no harm could come of allowing him to come over and at least see him. It's so obvious he's Tarim's, Maggie. Whatever Emma's said in the past.'

'So where do we go from here?' Maggie asked.

'I think you should meet him. I think the best way forward would be if you and Hannah came here and we all had a meeting. Emma and Tarim included. Discuss things properly. The thing is that Mike and I were talking and it seems to us that if these two plan on staying together – and the baby's going to be a part of that, obviously – then it makes sense to think of all three of them as a package, and work with them accordingly.'

'Let me speak with my manager,' Maggie said. 'I do see what you mean, absolutely. But it's a question of whether we're in a position to be able to do that. All we know about Tarim is what we've heard from Emma, obviously, and, as you know, none of that's terribly good, unfortunately. I tell you what, I'll call Hannah now, relate what you've told me – save you having to do it – and see if we can fix a time for

us both to come to you together. Then I'll speak to my manager. Give me a couple of hours and I'll get back to you.'

'Okay,' I said. 'Anything positive I can tell Emma in the meantime? She's obviously anxious …'

'Not yet, Casey. Let's just see what transpires first.'

I wasn't thrilled that I wouldn't be speaking to Hannah myself. I could imagine her and Maggie's conversation all too well. That and the thought process that would follow for Hannah. Baby in care. Her responsibility. Tarim out of prison. Emma flouncing off to see him against our wishes. Seeing Roman. Jailbird. Drug dealer. Jailbird. Drug dealer. Does-not-compute.

But much as I would have liked to frame things in language that wouldn't sound quite so damning, I didn't want to push it. And who knew, perhaps if Hannah actually met Tarim she might feel differently, just as I had. She might at least feel more inclined to give the pair of them a smidgen of a chance to prove they could be responsible parents. Well, I could only live in hope, couldn't I? I went back into the living room, plastering an optimistic smile on my face as I did so.

Emma looked up from where she was sitting, cross-legged on the floor. She'd been multi-tasking, clearly – texting someone one handed, while the other tickled Roman's tummy as he played on his play mat at her side.

I assumed the someone might be Tarim, but I was wrong. It was Tash.

'What did she say?' Emma asked me, once again without any attitude. No eye-rolling, scowling or other similar indicators that whatever anyone at social services said would be bad.

'She's going to have a chat with her manager, and we're going to set up a meeting,' I told her. 'All of us – you, me and Hannah –'

But Emma was only half listening as a new text came in. 'What day?' she wanted to know. 'Because I was wondering if I could text Tash back – tell her I can take Roman into town with her on Saturday. She's taking her little cousin and we thought we could all meet up. Her baby's due soon, too, so I said I'd help her choose some baby stuff. And I promise, Casey – we won't be going anywhere near Tarim …'

'I didn't imagine you *would* be,' I said, smiling. 'Not after last night's malarkey, missy. No, I don't imagine it will be on Saturday. Probably next week some time.'

I sat down on the sofa. Since she'd brought Tarim up, I thought I might too.

'So,' I said, 'what's Tarim up to now he's out? Does he have some work lined up? A plan? What's he doing with himself?'

She finished her text, threw the phone down, then pulled Roman to his feet. He loved her doing that now; letting him bounce on his chubby legs, loved to feel the weight of them. Before we knew it he'd be crawling and, soon after that, walking. And all hell would break loose once *that* happened.

'Right now?' Emma said. 'Sorting his flat out. He's going to the auctions with his dad Saturday, see if they can sort out some decent furniture.'

'He's staying there then, is he?' I asked her. 'From what I could see those flats looked almost derelict. Half of them didn't even seem to have windows.'

Emma pulled a face. She clearly agreed. 'It's horrible. I hate going there. It's really ropey. And he has to use tokens to get electricity. And he's got no money most of the time now so it's always dark, and there's no heating either. But only one of the windows is broken, and at least he has a sofa bed,' she added.

I shook my head, wondering quite how the place she described could ever be considered a suitable place for a baby to come visit. I was no snob – I'd been brought up on a council estate myself – but the thought of having to live in one of those flats made me shudder. Talk about grim sixties concrete jungle. They were like going back in time fifty years.

Still, I thought, as I chivvied Emma to get showered and dressed and ready, at least he had somewhere to live. And he was getting furniture with his dad, which meant his dad was engaged, which was a positive. He was at least trying.

When the phone rang a couple of hours later, I naturally assumed it would be Maggie. But it wasn't. It was John Fulshaw. Had Maggie been in overdrive? Was he already in the picture too?

'I've been speaking to Maggie,' he confirmed, answering my unspoken question. 'And Hannah Greenwood,' he added, 'and my manager.'

'That sounds promising,' I said, gauging from his tone that things looked positive. 'Do we have a verdict on things, then?'

'Not quite that,' he said. 'But it looks like we do have a trial of sorts, planned. To which end, we need to organise a full planning meeting. I know it's short notice, but we'd like both you and Mike to attend, and if it's in any way possible, for it to happen on Monday.'

'Wow, that *is* fast,' I said.

'And Emma and Tarim as well. Obviously. And Tarim's father, too.'

'His father?' This was particularly good news. Though Tarim was an adult, social services wouldn't consider him a responsible adult, not with him just having come out of prison for a drug-related offence.

'Yes,' John confirmed, 'they've already tracked him down too. Which isn't too surprising …' he chuckled. 'Tarim's already in the system, of course, due to other misdemeanours – been dealing a while, this kiddo – and he knows he hasn't a cat in hell's chance of being allowed contact unless dad steps up to the plate and gets involved as well. Which he is apparently prepared to do. I don't think they're a bad family, particularly. Dad's all right, I'm told. Just got a bit of a handful in the case of this particular son. But, yes, they're both agreeable and, well, all credit to the lad now at least he seems engaged with the process. So that's a positive, isn't it?'

One of many, I hoped. And I was glad to hear that Tarim came from an okay sort of a family – that he wasn't part of some dreadful criminal gang. 'It sure is,' I agreed. 'And that's a coincidence, as well. I was only talking to Emma about Tarim's dad earlier. Sounds like they're taking all this seriously, then, yes?'

'Oh, without a doubt,' John agreed. 'So you think Mike will be able to do Monday?'

'Oh, I'm sure he can. It'll only be a half day off. They'll be fine. So, when and where? Here as usual?'

'No, not this time. Given the circumstances we thought it best to opt for a neutral location. We don't really know enough about Tarim or his dad to have them invading your and Mike's privacy. So here at the office, we thought, if that works for you. Hannah's going to liaise with Tarim and his dad.'

'Brilliant,' I said. The day was shaping up better than I'd expected. 'But, off the record, do you have any idea what might happen next? What the plan actually is?'

'Not exactly,' John said, chuckling. 'So you'll have to hold your horses. But I think we're all of a mind where Tarim is concerned. If he's going to be on the scene now – and it seems he is, doesn't it? – then better that we're all involved in what happens in regard to Roman than his having free rein and keeping us all at arm's length.'

'Which is more or less what I said to Maggie. That's great, John,' I said. 'And it also shows Emma that she's being listened to,' I added. 'That we're trying to accommodate her wishes, which puts the ball very firmly in her court.'

And Tarim's, of course. And he was an adult. Fingers crossed he could go on to actually prove it.

After an incident-free weekend, Monday morning saw us all dashing around like idiots trying to get ready at the same time, as well as making sure Roman was fed, bathed and togged up in his Sunday best. As usual, I insisted that we couldn't leave until everything was tidied up, which had Emma and Mike raising their eyebrows at each other and adopting a conspiratorial 'we might as well just humour her and get on with it' kind of look. Emma was beginning to get to know me like Mike did by now. I knew I wouldn't operate at my best at the meeting unless I was relatively stress-free, and being stress-free was achieved by cleaning. So we cleaned.

We reached the fostering agency office with five minutes to spare. I'd not been down there in a long time, because there was hardly any need these days. I could probably count my visits in the last couple of years on the fingers of one hand. It felt a very long time since the day I'd pitched up there all those years back. It had been a day – and a meeting – that had profoundly changed my life.

Today, I hoped the same would apply to the three young lives we were here to talk about, and as we all went in I got my first inkling that it might. And that was because I barely recognised Tarim. It obviously *was* him, sitting in the waiting area beside the man who must be his father, but I still did a double take as I took him in. Gone were the baggy jeans hanging halfway down his backside and the elderly biker jacket. In their place I took in smart black trousers, off-white shirt, skinny tie, proper shoes. He was also nicely groomed, freshly shaved, and sported the sort of shiny hair that, were he my Kieron, I wouldn't have been able to resist ruffling.

Both Tarim and his father stood up, in unison. 'Billy Salazar,' the older man said, proffering a hand to Mike and then to me. 'Nice to meet you.' His smile was warm, his handshake firm, his face open – not to mention rather handsome. It was clear where Tarim had inherited his boyish good looks. So far, so good, I thought, glancing past him through the glass conference room doors.

The posse was all assembled, John already coming out to greet us. 'Come on in,' he said, reaching out to take Roman's car seat from Emma. 'Does he eat biscuits yet?' he asked her, grinning. 'For, today, we have biscuits. Even chocolate ones!' he added, winking at me.

'That means we're *really* honoured,' I quipped to Emma, making my way to a place round the huge conference table. In truth I felt almost as intimidated as I could see she was feeling. I'd never been much of a one for big, formal occasions – and these kinds of meetings, such a big part of the process in the care system, were exactly that, however many biscuits they laid on.

Still, once we'd got through the silly business of formally introducing ourselves to one another, I settled down a bit, and grew more focused on what might be about to come. First up was the lengthy business of filling in the background to the situation – though we had all been in touch since day one about how things had been progressing, it made sense to pull all the various threads together – particularly for the benefit of Tarim and his father who were obviously new to the whole process.

Hannah then went on to explain that, for the purpose of the meeting as well as any plans that were made as a result of it, it was going to be assumed that, contrary to what Emma had said when first placed into care, Tarim was, in fact, Roman's biological father.

'Will this create repercussions?' Tarim's father asked, very sensibly, I thought.

'Not at all,' Hannah reassured him. 'There's no question of there being action taken. It's obvious to everyone that Emma and Tarim are in a relationship and there's no evidence of coercion of any kind.'

That out of the way, Hannah explained that if Tarim and his father were to be allowed to have contact with Roman, they would both need to be police checked, and that everyone was aware of Tarim's recent spell in prison. She went on to say that he would have to work hard to prove that he could be a responsible partner to Emma and father to Roman and to that end would have to agree to attend parenting classes.

Tarim took this in and agreed to it unhesitatingly. I was also pleased to see the glances he and Emma had exchanged throughout this. There was a level of closeness and mutual support here that was obvious to everyone who saw it, and when he shyly outlined how he was looking for work now, and about his and his dad's plans for doing up his flat, I could sense the whole mood of the meeting shift and lighten.

Not that I tucked the cynical part of myself out of sight for the duration. That part of me was chirruping away in my ear even now, telling me not to get too carried away by this all-new and improved Tarim. I was fully aware of the person he could be, but I wasn't about to forget that this side of his personality was probably how he managed to manipulate Emma so easily.

Maggie spoke next. As Emma's social worker, she was responsible for looking after Emma's well-being, she explained. And to that end she agreed that Tarim having contact with both her and Roman would support that. 'So we're happy to put in place supervised contact,' she told Tarim and Emma. 'To take place at a family centre that's close to where you live, Tarim, and also, as long as Casey and Mike are happy to agree to it, at their house too – as long as it's pre-arranged and they're at home.'

We both agreed. In fact we welcomed it, because it represented a great leap forward. Far better to welcome him into our home and get to know him and support them both with Roman than have her sneaking around trying to see him without us knowing.

Then finally, finally, it was Emma's turn to speak, when Maggie asked her how she felt about what was being proposed. 'Do you have anything to add,' Maggie wanted to know, 'about what you would like to happen?'

And that's when Emma dropped her bombshell.

'Okay,' she began, 'well, first I really want to thank everybody ...' Good, I thought. She'd remembered our little chat and had obviously rehearsed it. 'I know I've messed up,' she went on. 'And I know I've been silly and a bit irresponsible, and I want to say thanks for giving me and Taz a chance to prove we can do okay. And ...' she paused and looked at Tarim, '... and, well, me and Taz were talking on the phone last night, and we were thinking ... well, there was something I wonder if I could ask you?'

She looked at Maggie, who nodded and smiled and beckoned for her to continue. 'Course you can,' she said. 'Anything. Anything you need ... anything that's worrying you ...'

Emma shook her head slightly. 'It's not anything that's worrying me, exactly. It's just about me and Roman moving into one of those mother and baby places. I was wondering if I *had* to do that – whether it was actually in the rules? Because it's just that –' she glanced at me now, then Mike, then back to Maggie. She was now blushing furiously. 'What I was wondering,' she said nervously, making me wonder what on earth was coming next, 'was if it would be possible for me to stay with Casey and Mike till I'm sixteen instead? I mean, I know I'm not mum of the year – actually, I'm pretty crap still, aren't I? And I just think,' she went on, the words tumbling out in a rush now, 'that if I stay with them I know I'll do much better than if I have to be on my own. I just ...' she shrugged then and looked right at me. 'Can I *please*, Casey?'

Now it was my turn to blush. I was stunned. Where had *that* come from? That would mean – when was her birthday? – another fourteen, fifteen months. A long time. A long *intense* time, moreover. With a baby who'd become a toddler ... It was a great deal to take in.

'My,' said John, clearly watching me and Mike struggling to do so, 'that's a bit out of the blue, Emma!' He grinned to reassure her. 'You know,' he went on, 'that's really quite a big thing to spring on us, not only because Mike and Casey will need a bit of time to think about it, but also because, as you know, they're part of my specialist fostering team. They're not strictly speaking trained as mother and baby carers – they only got that status temporarily so they could step in and help out and look after you. So I think what's best is if we all –'

'Yes,' I said, 'we'll do it.'

I didn't need to consult with Mike because our hands had already consulted, under the table. He squeezed mine now. 'I'm sorry,' I said to John, 'that is, of course, if it's all right with you.'

'Casey, you really don't need to make this decision now,' John cautioned. 'I think we all of us need to think about something as big as this.'

'No we don't,' I said. 'At least, Mike and I don't. I mean, have your meeting, or whatever you need to do, but as far as we're concerned it's fine. If it's what Emma wants – and I happen to think that's very sensible of you, Emma – then Mike and I are fine with it. If we can, we will.'

Emma leapt out of her seat then, pushed her chair back and ran round to us. 'Oh thank you, thank you, thank you!' she said, hugging each of us in turn.

'Well, well,' said Mike, afterwards, while we sat in the car just down the high street, while Emma and Roman said a quick goodbye to Tarim and his dad.

'Well, well, indeed,' I agreed.

'Teenagers,' Mike observed. 'Never a dull moment with teenagers.'

'Or, indeed, toddlers,' I replied, smiling at the thought of my utter lunacy. I turned to Mike and grinned at him. 'And now we have both!'

'Bloody hell, Casey,' he said. 'You don't mess about, do you, love?'

'I know,' I said. 'I think I'm still a little bit in shock. Have we practically just gone and adopted a teenager and a six-month-old baby?'

'Seems that way,' he chuckled, shaking his head.

But the day wasn't done with surprises. I pulled my phone from my bag at that point, to switch it back on after the meeting, to find three missed calls from my daughter. Which prompted the inevitable moment of maternal panic. What had happened? What was the emergency? What was *wrong*? But there was also a voicemail, and as soon as I was two seconds into it – 'Mu-um! Where are you? Call me back this very instant!' – I could tell by Riley's jolly tone that there was no need to send for the cavalry. Instead I cut her off mid-flow, and called her instead.

So it was that, just as Emma was skipping back down the road to get in the car, she found me whooping and punching the air and generally acting the loony.

'Whattt?' she and Mike asked in unison, as she clambered in.

'Woo hoo!' I trilled, for want of a better word. 'Grandchild number three alert, folks – Riley's pregnant!'

Chapter 14

The next couple of weeks went by in something of a blur. First the development – which had taken some time to sink in – that we were going to care for Emma and Roman for another year and a half, then the brilliant but also unexpected news that Riley was to be a mum again. She'd said nothing – given me no inkling whatsoever – which seemed really out of character. We were so close. And I hadn't even realised they'd been trying.

But when I'd quizzed her, wondering if it was because I'd been so wrapped up in my fostering, Riley had laughed out loud. 'That's because we weren't, Mum, you nitwit!' she said. 'We'd hardly have been trying for a baby and going through the fostering application at the same time, would we?'

Which set my mind at rest. A happy accident, that was all.

So here we were, as a family, in completely new territory. Our own house now occupied long term by a teen and a tot, and a third grandchild due around Christmas.

'I feel old, Casey,' Mike said, peering into the dressing-table mirror, as he was getting ready for work a couple of Mondays later. He pulled a face. 'Really old. Look at all this grey coming through!'

I sprung from the bed. I felt curiously energised myself. 'Don't be daft,' I said. 'Keep you fit, all these little ones will. Mind you,' I added, noting how, despite my get-up and go, my back creaked as I did so, 'at the rate Riley and David are going, we'll soon have a bloody nursery full! Let's hope it's a girl, eh? And then may be that'll be the end of it.'

You could have too much of a good thing, after all. I grabbed my dressing gown. 'I'll go get showered while you get the coffee on,' I told him. 'Er … If that's not too much effort for you, old man!' I then added, which earned me a flick on the backside with the towel he'd been drying his hair with.

I would never admit it of course, and for the most part I was largely delighted, but as the days passed there was the odd moment when I had a small 'Oh, my, what have we done?' moment, and felt rather daunted by recent events. One thing kept coming back to me: would we have committed to keeping Emma and baby Roman if we'd had Riley's news before that particular meeting?

It would have given us pause for thought, certainly – how could it not have? But, try as I might, I couldn't decide if we'd have still reached the same decision. So I should do myself a favour, really, I kept telling myself, and stop trying to answer that particular question.

I was so thrilled for Riley, because she was so thrilled herself. What had been a delightful accident that we were all a bit bemused by had now changed into full-on excitement. Now she was expecting again she had allowed herself to nurture a definite hope for a little girl, or a 'pink one' as she so eloquently called it.

Less straightforward, and potentially more stressful, of course, was the formalising of our roles as mother and baby carers to Emma for the next year and a half. Though I relished the challenge, I was definitely a little apprehensive about guiding her. Roman was adorable, an easy baby – no trouble at all. But that was in my view – and it wasn't for me to bring him up. Social services had made that fact abundantly clear when they had sanctioned it, and John had spelled it out in no uncertain tones.

'Emma's the one that has to do the bringing up here, okay, Casey? You're there to guide her and help her to make the right decisions, but at the end of the day the doing of it is her job. Obviously, now you have mother and baby status, you also have full responsibility for both of them – which means you can override her decisions if you ever feel she's putting Roman at risk in any way, and take charge if you feel it's warranted and needed. But if that happens then you must always call Maggie, Hannah or myself, and cover your back by keeping detailed notes on everything. I'm not telling you how to suck eggs,' he had finished, grinning at me, 'but it's important to me that you and Mike are properly protected – you know?'

I did know. This was obviously a great deal more complex than having responsibility for a single young child. I now had two, and if what was good for one wasn't good for the other … Well, I just hoped it was a bridge I didn't need to cross.

So far, happily, everything seemed to be going to plan. Emma was ecstatic that Tarim was officially allowed back into her life, and now he was no longer her guilty little secret she opened up more. She was also much more biddable and happy to be cooperative, skipping off to her 'school' eagerly – and not just because I was the childcare, because she seemed to genuinely be blossoming. The dark days of her mother's letter and being told she was a piece of rubbish seemed just that – dark days, that were long behind us. She didn't mention her mother and neither did I. It was all about looking forward, to Roman's development, to being with Tarim – to a future that looked like being so much better than the past.

As for me, I was in full-on Casey overdrive. With Roman now seven months old and crawling – not to mention exercising his newly found baby-gabble voice – my germ busting had gone into overdrive. I found myself constantly spraying and wiping – any surface his little hands might reach. It did wonders for my skirting boards and surfaces, obviously, but nothing for my poor creaky back.

By the time Tarim had his first official contact visit at our house, I had even begun to allow myself to ignore the little voice that kept whispering that I should be braced for the next disaster. Able to see Tarim on her own now, Emma was just so much happier in every way, and the successful contact visits the three of them had enjoyed at the family centre had convinced all of us the time was right to have Tarim visit at our house, so that they could all bond in a less official environment. And though I naturally had to supervise, I felt able to relax the reins.

In fact, having been so touched to see how well Tarim was bonding with his infant son, I allowed them to have the living room to themselves.

'Are you sure?' Emma asked. 'I mean don't you or Mike actually have to be in the room with us or something?' Which in itself reassured us – it was clear she was taking the rules seriously now.

'Well, yes, if I was doing it by the letter, then I would be,' I told her and Tarim, 'but I do want the three of you to be able to spend some time alone. I tell you what,' I said, conscious that I still needed to maintain a presence, 'I'll just be in either the kitchen or the dining-room area, so if we leave the door open I can still sort of supervise, can't I? I'll be able to hear you but I won't be so in your face. Give you a degree of privacy.'

And, in fact, I could hear everything and see plenty anyway. Tarim helped dress Roman, then took charge of giving him lunch, which had Emma in fits of laughter as he sat there carefully starting to pull tiny pieces from a sandwich, while Roman banged his chubby fists down impatiently.

'He can do it himself, Taz,' she giggled. 'Just leave the two halves on the tray, see? He can manage perfectly well. You just have to watch he doesn't try to stuff the whole lot in at once – which he will if you keep him hanging about waiting much longer!'

Tarim looked completely amazed at this development. Giving Roman the sandwich, he shook his head. 'I can't believe I've got a kid who can already feed himself!' he marvelled. 'I've missed so much, Ems. Hey, he's going to be well clever, isn't he?'

It was a joy to watch them, and even if they did look a bit like two kids playing at being mummy and daddy, that was as much about me as it was about them. Once you were my age everyone under about twenty-five looked a bit kid-like, I supposed. But whatever my thoughts about their youth, things were falling into place now; things were just so much calmer, in all respects, too – Tarim seemed to have a really positive influence on Emma's state of mind. Roman was happy too, as kids always are when their mums are happy. Life was drama-free, and that was just the way I liked it.

But what you like isn't always what you get. On the Friday after Tarim's visit, just before heading off for school, Emma asked if she could meet up with him after school. 'Only he's been and got a cot and a mobile and everything, ready for when we're allowed to go for a sleepover. And they've been decorating and everything, him and his dad … And it'll only be for a bit – I'll be back by five-thirty, promise.'

A Last Kiss for Mommy

I had no problem with Emma and Tarim meeting by now, obviously, just as long as it suited me – I was always the babysitter, after all – and as long as she didn't push the boundaries. So far she hadn't, so there was no reason to object. Though what I didn't say was that Roman would more likely need a bed than a cot by the time Emma and he were allowed to stay over at Tarim's. And no longer be in my care, for that matter, as until she was sixteen there was no way social services would sanction it.

'Go on, then,' I said, pleased that he was evidently planning for their futures. 'I'm sure you're dying to see it, aren't you? And you can have till six, but not a minute longer, because by then you'll have to take over. I'll have had Roman all day by then and will need to start preparing Mike's tea. Okay?'

She threw her skinny arms around me, her ponytail swinging as she embraced me. 'Oh, thank you, thank you!' she said, skipping off to start her day. And me mine. I pushed my sleeves up and began my daily clock watch. If I'd forgotten how much you have to plan your day when you've got a baby to look after, I had remembered now, all too well – *lots*!

I had just put Roman down for his afternoon nap when Riley walked in; come to visit for a catch-up and a coffee and a sit-down, before picking Levi and Jackson up from school. 'Oh,' she said, casting around and finding Roman absent from downstairs, 'is he asleep? I should have left it till a bit later, shouldn't I?'

'Charming!' I scolded her. 'I thought it was me you'd come to visit! We're both so flipping busy these days and when you do show up to see me I find it's not even me you've come to see!'

Riley pulled me in for a hug. 'Of course it's you I've come to see,' she reassured me. 'I was just after a bit of baby-cuddling practice. It's been a while now …'

'Oh, you'll be getting plenty of that soon enough,' I said. 'Though have you told the agency?' I asked her. 'I was thinking about that the other day. No sooner have you been passed than you can't actually do it! And you've only just got under way!'

She shook her head. 'Not yet. It's a bit early to start doing that stuff. But we've talked – David and I, that is – and we're not really bothered. With being respite carers it's not like the pregnancy will affect too much – not till the end, at least – so we thought we'd crack on for the time being and see how it goes.'

Riley and David were now the proud veterans of their first respite foster placement, having looked after a twelve-year-old girl a few months earlier, just for the weekend, and found the whole experience nothing but positive. And there was no reason why they couldn't continue for the time being – it would all be great experience under their belts.

Before I knew it, it was time for Roman to be brought down from his nap and, once Riley had gone – the cuddle completed – and I'd given him a snack and got him changed, there was only an hour or so before Emma was due back home. I filled it with a little more housework while Roman sat and watched me, swapping places with Mike when he came in at five-thirty.

Even though I'd said six, when it got to ten to I could feel myself counting the minutes off. Silly, given the past few weeks, but even so I couldn't shake it – it was just too important, I supposed, for me not to. So when the door went at five to I mentally exhaled. Good girl. And good Tarim, as well. But even as I turned on a tap to rinse my hands so I could go out into the hall to greet her, I heard the door slam, followed by footsteps thundering straight up the stairs.

That felt odd; if she needed the loo, she'd use the one in the hall, surely? Mike wasn't in there. He was on the living-room floor, playing trains with Roman – I could hear him. I came out into the hall at the same time as he did, baby in arms. 'Was that Emma?' he asked me.

'I think so,' I said, the slam of the door fresh in my ears. 'You stay with Roman. I'll nip up and see what's wrong.'

When I got to the top of the stairs I could hear water running and was relieved to see the bathroom door was open. I went in to find Emma splashing water on her face, holding her hair back as she did so, head bent close to the sink.

'Are you all right, love?' I asked her, as she continued to cup her hand and keep refilling it. She wasn't answering. 'Emma?' I said. 'Emma, what is it, love?'

Now she did turn, and what I saw made me catch my breath. She'd obviously been crying, but that was the least of it. Her lip was bleeding and swollen and it looked like one of her eyes was swelling so rapidly it was starting to be sealed shut. It was livid, and it looked like it was grazed as well.

'Oh my God!' I exclaimed, covering the two strides between us. 'What's happened to you?'

She twisted away from me slightly as I tried to place my hands on her shoulders so I could get a better look at her face. 'Oh, Casey, I'm *fine*,' she rebuked me, as if I was a child, and she was an adult – and that I was making a big fuss over nothing. Perhaps her vision was impaired – could she see how bad she looked?

'Fine?' I gaped.

'Yes,' she said. 'It was just a little fight –'

'Little fight?' I said. 'With who exactly?'

I spent a millisecond allowing for the hopeful possibility that this was some spat with a girl at the unit. Which would still be bad, but not half as bad as my next thought. 'Was this Tarim?' I asked her, horrified. 'Did Tarim do this to you?'

'Yes, of course it was Tarim,' she said irritably, cutting off the hope before it even had a chance to root.

She turned back to the sink then and returned to bathing her swollen eye with water. 'I just need to keep putting cold water on it,' she said matter-of-factly. Then she looked at herself closely in the bathroom cabinet mirror. 'Fucking men,' she said quietly, more in sorrow than in anger as she gingerly prodded at it. 'They're all the fucking same, Casey, aren't they?'

I couldn't believe what I was hearing – definitely couldn't believe the tone in which I was hearing it. Couldn't believe that that innocent-looking, charming-looking, lovely-looking boy – that boy who I'd *completely* changed my mind about, damn him – had just done the ugliest thing imaginable to this girl.

'Tarim did this to you?' I said again. 'Punched you? Tarim hit you?'

'I told you,' she said, lowering her head and returning to the splashing. 'We had a fight –'

'Oh, so he has an eye that looks like that too, does he?'

'I *wish*,' she said, with a degree of vehemence from behind her curtain of hair. Then she lifted her head again and sighed. 'What?' she said, meeting my eye and presumably shocked by my horrified expression. 'You're not telling me you've never come across a bit of domestic violence, are you? Christ, it's not like he's the only bloke to have ever given his bird a smack, is it? Just leave it, Casey, okay. I'll be fine.'

I was stunned. She was fourteen and she was talking like she was forty. The sort of forty-year-old often attached to a big glass of mother's ruin down the pub, having spent the best years of her life being smacked around by men. A prostitute, a drug user – more often than not, both. So while I was set on finding out all the whats and whys and wherefores, I was more concerned, in the short term, about Emma's attitude towards it – that this sort of thing was perfectly normal. It took my breath away.

'I'm sorry, Emma,' I said, trying to keep my voice level, 'I won't be leaving it.' The last thing I wanted was to have the volume ballooning the way the skin around her eye seemed to be doing.

'Please?' she said wearily. '*Please*? It will all be okay if you just *leave* it.'

'No it won't. How do you work that out? In what sense well it "be okay" exactly? Okay for who? You? I'm afraid I don't get that. Who the hell does he think he is, anyway? Is he mad? You realise he could go straight back to prison if you report what he's done to you? Do you?'

She stopped filling her hand again and shook the drips from it angrily. 'Grass him up?' she spluttered. 'Grass on my own boyfriend? Are you for *real*? It was just a little argument that got a bit heated. That was *all*. I've told you, I'll be *fine*. Christ, it's like, nothing! Are you for real?' she said again. 'Look,' she added, 'I really need to pee, okay. Can I, like, do *that* at least? Please?'

'Should we call someone?' Mike asked once I trooped back downstairs. He was in the hallway, presumably having heard much of our exchange, Roman grizzling and fretful in his arms now. 'John?' he went on. 'Maggie? The police? We can't just leave this.'

I shook my head. 'Not just yet,' I said. 'Not till we get a few answers. Once anyone else is involved she'll just clam right up, I know it. Let's just see what we can get out of her first.'

Emma came down, moments later, looking guarded and slightly sullen, as if it were I who'd offended her most in this equation by having the temerity to speak ill of Tarim.

She immediately set about sorting Roman's tea out, pulling a jar of baby food from the cupboard and opening the microwave, then pulling his high chair close to the kitchen table, ready.

That done, she took Roman from Mike without a word or gesture, sat him in the chair and, while he began welly-ing in to his jar of chicken dinner, started chopping bits of banana for his pudding.

'Look,' she said to both of us, in the same world-weary air, 'it's not what you think, okay? It's not.'

Since neither of us answered – we were too gobsmacked – she sighed and tried again. 'Look,' she said, 'I know it seems weird if you've never seen it before, but Tarim loves me, okay. He really didn't mean to do this. Look, he's sorry, okay? And if it's any consolation, he feels *terrible*. Look, I can handle it –' she looked at me. 'Honestly. I can handle it, and I can handle him. God, this is *nothing* –'

Mike rolled his eyes. I could see he knew exactly how he'd handle Tarim, given half a chance. 'Nothing compared to what?' he asked her pointedly.

'Nothing compared to the sort of shit my mother had to put up with. Take anything from anyone, *she* would. That's not *me*! This is just relationship stuff, okay. It *happens*. Look,' Emma said again, while I tried to stop my eyes bulg-ing out of their sockets, 'I'm not trying to defend him, okay? I wouldn't do that. But sometimes these things, well – they just happen. You can't go off on one just because of one fight –'

'It wasn't a fight,' I said. 'He *hit* you.'

'Yeah, but I started it.'

'Emma, love,' Mike started, 'I'm sorry, but that's a load of crap. Like Casey says, it wasn't a fight – not a fair fight. He's a fully grown man, Emma, and he *hit* you. He's bigger than you and stronger than you and any way you choose to describe it, it's abuse, plain and simple. Like I heard you say, it's domestic violence, but the emphasis is very much on the "violence" bit, and no matter how you dress it up, or try to tone it down, he deserves to be punished.'

I could see the tears welling in Emma's eyes – well, the one eye that wasn't swollen anyway. 'Don't you think he *knows* that?' she railed at Mike, as if she was the counsel for the defence in court. 'Don't you think he's suffering now, cos of this? He's devastated, he is, *devastated*. And it's not even his fault!'

I could tell from the way Mike was clenching and unclenching his fingers that he was getting angry, and I didn't want him to lose his cool. I needed to intervene. 'Okay, love,' I said gently, 'if that's how you feel then you must explain why you say that. Make us understand. Why was this not really Tarim's fault?'

But Emma shook her head. 'What's the point?' she said, obviously seeing Mike's set expression. She wasn't stupid. 'You want to blame him. How can you understand, living the sort of lives you live? Your perfect lives, your perfect kids, your perfect *everything*. You have no idea about *real* life at all!'

'This *is* real life,' I corrected her. 'And trust me, we have seen some. And we're not perfect – never were – and neither are our kids. So I don't know where you get the idea that we can't understand this. I know all about violence and "domestic violence", as you call it – and it's still violence. What I can't understand is how you can sit there and be so loyal to someone who has punched you in the face. *That's* what I don't get.' I waited just a heartbeat.

'Because I love him! And he loves me, and he never meant to hurt me. Can't you get that? It was his mate!'

Mike scoffed. 'His *mate* that hit you? Come on, Emma, don't pull –'

'No, not hit me!' she barked back at him. 'He told him shit about me! He told him I slept with his other mate while he was inside! I don't know why. Don't have a clue what the fuck he has against me. Probably jealous that Tarim's got a decent life in front of him. Probably jealous of me cos Tarim doesn't wanna get stoned with him all the time now – I don't know! But it was him. *Now* d'you see?'

'And did you?' I asked her.

'Did I what?'

'Did you sleep with this boy?'

She looked dumbfounded. 'Of course I didn't! Why the hell would I ever do that?' She exhaled heavily. 'But how could Tarim *know* that? He wasn't there, was he? And he trusts Kel – he's, like, his best mate – so he's bound to believe him, isn't he?'

'Over you?' asked Mike.

'No!' she said. Then seemed to think. 'But, yeah. Yeah, a bit. Of *course* he doubted me. He was bound to. Stuck inside. Me on the outside. Us not seeing each other. I totally get that! Why can't *you*?'

By now Roman was grizzling quietly, clearly as sick of the situation as we were. Emma snatched him up from his high chair, knocking the spoon onto the carpet, where it spread a small slick of curry-coloured puree.

'Look, you have no *idea*, okay?' she said, bending automatically to retrieve it. She seemed so small and frail, so innocent, so fragile – especially with the now hefty Roman parked on her hip. How dare he. How bloody *dare* he. I was quietly seething.

'Go upstairs,' Mike said, his voice thankfully controlled and measured now. 'Sort out Roman, get him ready for bed. We can talk about this later on.'

I reached an arm out and squeezed Emma's. This time she didn't pull away from me. 'Go on, love,' I said. 'Like Mike said, we'll talk later.'

'There's nothing to talk *about*,' she insisted, loyal to the very last, as she left the room.

I shook my head sadly. She was so wrong. There *was*.

Chapter 15

I woke the next morning with a splitting headache. I hadn't had one in a long while and I didn't doubt this one was due mostly to tension. The memories of the previous evening came rushing in to join it. We'd got no further with Emma even though we'd tried the softly-softly tactic. She was adamant; it was completely understandable that Tarim had lost it, and even if she was cross with him – which she did concede she still was – she was resolutely forgiving and loyal.

I got up, feeling sluggish as I turned on the shower, weighed down by the prospect of a difficult day. As well as the couple of painkillers I threw down, I knew I would need plenty of caffeine to get through the morning.

'So,' said Mike, once I was downstairs and dressed, 'you're going to make some calls this morning, are you? Report this?' He was heading off to work for the morning before returning at lunchtime, ready for his Saturday afternoon football with Kieron. I wished I could go with him.

Just throw a coat on and go. And I never felt like that about my work.

He passed me coffee. 'Give me a moment, love,' I chided as I took it from him. 'Of course I am. I must. But I'm not going to do it just yet. I really don't want to till I'm sure Emma understands why we *have* to.'

'Good luck with that,' he observed, managing a smile to go with it. Albeit a grim one. We both knew the potential implications of reporting Tarim's violence. And neither of us felt up to facing them.

'I know,' I said, sighing. 'But I at least want to try first. If I can just get her to see that he needs to address this sort of behaviour – God, even if just because she needs to think about protecting Roman – then I'll feel much happier about doing it, that's all.'

I sat down at the kitchen table and Mike sat down with me. 'Casey, love,' he said gently, 'look, I know it's going to be hard, but truth be told, it really shouldn't be. We should be clear what our roles are. If we let it go this time –' he raised a hand. 'No, I know you're not *saying* that, but part of you is thinking that, I know it is – then it's absolutely as if we're condoning this. It would send exactly the wrong message to Emma, you know that. Thanks to that mother of hers, she already thinks it's okay to get the odd slap off a man, God help that woman. She clearly never fought back, never told her daughter it was unacceptable – just sucked it up, took it on the chin, literally. And it's a cycle that will just keep repeating in perpetuity if we – you and me – don't nip it straight in the bud.'

I knew Mike was right. Of course he was. That was our job. But I also knew myself, and while he'd been talking I'd been thinking, and it was becoming clearer by the moment what was really rattling me. It was this endless need to play bad cop – having to be the person who 'ruined everything' – as Emma had pointed out I would most definitely be if I made a phone call and grassed Tarim up.

I knew Mike understood because I could see it in his face, but actually this wasn't about hurting my feelings, was it? It was just so much more important than that.

Emma didn't come down till about ten, and when she did – Roman balanced on her hip, his usual sunny self – she was subdued and looked tired. Perhaps, with the benefit of some time having passed now, we'd be able to discuss things more calmly.

'Say hi to Casey,' she said to Roman as they came into the kitchen. He was smiling and holding his arms out towards me. I didn't take him from her; instead I held up the coffee pot. She shook her head.

'I'll just have milk, thanks,' she said. She was lisping.

I put the jug down and came closer. Her face looked terrible. Worse than last night, even, her left eye fully closed now, and her lip, also swollen, competing with the eye socket for which would create the most colourful bruising.

'Oh, Emma,' I said. 'Just look at your face, love. You know,' I said, peering closer, anxious about the bits I couldn't see, 'I think we might need to see the doctor with that eye.'

193

Now I did take Roman from her, because he was struggling to get to me, and popped him in his high chair so I could get her a glass of milk.

'Don't fuss, Casey,' she said to me. 'I told you, I'm fine. I've had a black eye before and I'll probably have one again. Few days, it'll be gone.'

Given what had happened the previous evening, what she said didn't shock me. But I clearly needed to try a different tack.

'That's the thing, though, you see, love. I'm paid to fuss, aren't I? Paid to care – paid to look after you and Roman. Do you really think for an instant that I can leave this thing? Do you? Love, why can't you see that this is wrong?'

And so it began. Another full-scale row, just as we'd had the previous evening, with me telling Emma I'd be reporting Tarim's violence and her telling me that I had no right to do that and that I might as well just kill her as I was going to ruin her life.

I tried. I tried to make her see that the 'rules' she'd grown up with – that women annoyed men, which meant men couldn't help but hit them – were wrong on every single level imaginable. 'Don't you see, Emma?' I pleaded. 'It's a pattern – a terrible pattern. You watched it happen to your mother; watched her let men abuse her and hurt her, and because she let them you now think it's normal. But think back. Think back to when you were a little girl and you saw that violence happen. And to your mum, your own mum, who you loved. How did it make you feel then? Terrified, I'm guessing. You must have hated it. Hated it. Is that what you want for Roman? To watch as his father gives his mum a black eye?'

But it was pointless, as it had been for some women in perpetuity, and would be again in the future. Because her argument was the same that was used by women every-where – most frequently the broken women holed up in battered women's refuges, having used it, to their detri-ment, for years.

'But it's not like that!' she persisted. 'Tarim's not like those dickheads! They were just scumbags – one-night stands, wasters – they didn't love her. They couldn't give a toss, but Tarim's different. Tarim loves me! Why can't you get that through your head?'

'Okay,' I said, feeling my temper taking hold of me. 'Here's Roman. Who you love. And he does something to annoy you. At what point do you think it's going to be a valid course of action to raise your fist – given that he's smaller than you, younger than you, weaker than you – to raise that fist and slam it into *his* face? Emma, we don't hurt the people we love! And for that matter, according to your "can't help it" logic, what's to stop Tarim punching Roman in the face?'

'Don't be stupid, Casey!' she spat back at me. 'He'd never do that! And he'd never have hit me in front of the baby. I'd *never* allow that!'

'Allow?' Now I was incredulous. 'You think you could stop him? If you could stop him doing anything you wouldn't be sitting here right now with a fat lip and an eye you can't open!'

Emma stood then. 'You're wrong, Casey. Wrong, wrong, wrong, wrong. Tarim would never hurt Roman, not in a million zillion years. And the only reason he hit me was because he loves me so much. No, he shouldn't have done, but you only do stuff like that if you really, really, *really* love a person!'

She stormed out then, slamming the door, leaving poor Roman staring after her and leaving me reeling, hot and shaking, in her wake.

Perhaps because he sensed it was a shrewd move under the circumstances, Mike called an hour or so later. Given the time, he said, he'd go straight from the warehouse to meet with Kieron, and would be back at teatime, to get the 'next episode of the soap opera on catch-up'. It was an attempt to lighten my mood and, to some extent, it was a good one. There were deep issues to address here, and – *make no mistake*, I thought – I would bloody well address them, but there was also the issue of having a fourteen-year-old girl in the house. Shouting and slamming doors were par for the course. I mustn't lose my sense of perspective.

By this time I had already decided I would telephone John Fulshaw, just as soon as Roman went down for his nap. I went through what I'd say while sitting on a patio chair in the garden, collecting my thoughts while Roman played happily in his playpen, which I'd taken out and set up on the grass. Of Emma herself, there hadn't a peek since she'd stormed out of the kitchen, just the low thunks and lunks of her CD player going, playing whatever tunes were proving balm to her troubled mind. And, for the moment, I was happy that she stay in her room.

But apparently there was someone else who wasn't.

Roman had just fallen asleep, right there, in the sun, on his play mat on the lawn, when I heard shouting from out in the street. It was being carried in on the breeze, over the side fence that led to the front garden, and at first I thought I must have imagined it. It was a sleepy sunny Saturday afternoon in a residential neighbourhood, but, no, there it was again, somebody yelling. And being very free with their language, too, which made me stop in my tracks. I'd been just about to go and call John, so was putting a blanket over Roman, and though he didn't wake – he was the sort of baby who could readily sleep through anything – I imagined half the street coming out.

I shot inside and went straight to the living-room window, where I was horrified to see Tarim, leaning on our wall. He had a bottle of what looked like cider, which he was swinging from one hand, and was shouting up towards our bedroom windows. 'Get down here, you fucking slag!' he roared. 'Come on, what's the fucking matter? Nothing to say, eh?'

Two things were clear. One that he was very, very drunk and, two, that the 'fucking slag' in question was Emma. I rushed out into the hall and shouted up at her to come downstairs immediately. She appeared on the landing, looking sheepish.

'Don't let him in,' she warned. 'Not in that state. He'll kill us.'

I could still hear him – clearly – still entreating so delightfully, and, in between, shouting at what presumably were neighbours, asking them what they 'thought they were fucking looking at'. I was mortified. We'd already had to move once because of our fostering activities, and these neighbours, like most of the last, were all such lovely, decent people. They really didn't deserve this. And shouldn't have to.

'I can't wait all day!' Tarim roared again. 'Get out here and fucking face me!' Then, obviously to someone who'd dared to face up to him. 'Get in, you fucking nosey old bag,' he railed. 'So ring the fucking police – see if I care!'

Emma came halfway down the stairs, then sat down abruptly, as, fed up with things now, I reached for the door handle. 'You're not going to let him in, are you?' she squeaked at me. 'Don't let him in, Casey – please don't!'

'Oh, don't you worry,' I reassured her, wondering where her bravado about Tarim had suddenly disappeared to. 'I've taken on far worse than him in my time, Emma. If he tries to cross me he'll know about it.'

It was all bravado, but, fired up with mortification, I pulled the door open and stepped out onto the front path. 'Tarim?' He blinked at me, clearly struggling even to focus. 'She isn't coming out to talk to you. I'm not letting her. Not with you in that state. Go home, sober up, and when you think you can be civil you can come back again for a chat, if that's what you want. And do it *now*. I'm not having this, Tarim. You hear me? I am not having it.'

'Fuck off!' was his considered response. 'Just get that slut out here. I'm not shutting up and I'm not going away. I'm not doing neither,' he added, swaying against the front wall, 'till she comes out and tells me if it's true!'

'Just go,' I said, but now he was talking to another neighbour.

'You know what she said, mate?' he slurred at the poor man. 'She's a slag, she is. She said he's not even fucking mine! I'll do the DNA, you know.' He swung around again. 'I'll do the fucking DNA, you SLAG!'

I turned around. Emma was now sitting at the bottom of the stairs, crying.

'You told him that?' I hissed. 'That the baby wasn't his? That was clever.'

'He made me!' she said, sobbing. 'He was winding me up so much – I just wanted to say something to hurt him! I didn't mean it. I've never been with anyone – not ever …' She dropped her head into her hands and sobbed some more.

This was shaping up really well. 'Tarim!' I said, turning back to him. 'Look, last time of asking. Go home, sober up and we'll talk about this later. If you don't, you give me no choice but to call the police and –'

I had to stop speaking then and duck back inside, pretty sharpish, to avoid the cider bottle that was winging towards me and which had been thrown with such force and accuracy that it missed me by inches, smashing loudly against the front door.

'That's it,' I said, to an equally startled Emma. 'I've given him more than enough chances. I'm phoning the police.'

Emma leapt to her feet then. 'Oh, please don't, Casey. *Please* don't do that. He'll be so sorry when he sobers up. He'll be just horrified. He'll buy you flowers and everything, I know he will. I promise, Casey, he doesn't know what he's on about just now. You can see that, can't you?'

She was actually gripping my arm now. I felt sick. She was completely taken in by this lad, it was clear. Hook, line and sinker. She really did believe the rubbish that was currently spewing from her mouth. Flowers? *Flowers?* It beggared belief.

I shook my head. 'I'm sorry, love,' I said, 'but not a chance, I'm afraid. You might be happy to, but I'm not taking this sort of crap from anyone. No, I'm sorry but I'm going to go and do what I should have done first thing this morning. Because maybe if I had, then he wouldn't be here now shouting the odds at us both, would he? Now go and check on Roman, will you? It'll be a miracle if he managed to sleep through that. He's out in the garden. Go on. Scoot.'

She duly did.

They didn't take long. Within a matter of minutes we were back stationed by the window, watching a burly police officer and policewoman escorting Tarim to their patrol car. Once he was inside, the policewoman came indoors to take a statement, while such neighbours as had stayed out to watch the closing scenes of this short and sorry drama went back inside, presumably to gossip about quite who the drunken thug was.

It was left to me to explain, as Emma cried for the duration, and when the policewoman asked about her facial injuries and I urged her to explain them she refused, saying that it was just a bit of horseplay that had got out of hand and that she wouldn't be pressing any charges.

'It's up to you, lovey,' the policewoman said, flipping her little pad closed, 'but I can assure you, if he's hit you once, then he'll hit you again.' She paused and glanced at me, then back at Emma. 'It never, ever stops at "just the once", love. Ask anyone who's been there.'

But her words were falling on deaf ears and both of us could see that. So she left, and as soon as she was walking down the path Emma rounded on me, teary-eyed, again. 'If he ends up back inside,' she said, jabbing her index finger towards me, 'and leaves Roman without his daddy, then I'm holding you responsible, because it will all have been your fault!'

Yes, I was angry. Yes, I was aghast. Yes, I was traumatised by what had happened, but at the same time I could so clearly see her pain. She just didn't get it. This was par for the course, this was normal, this was the way it was in relationships. And it was that which was set to be her downfall. I sighed and walked back outside to check again on Roman. He had slept through everything. The whole sorry business.

'Look, I'm sorry, love,' I said, as she followed me into the garden, 'but he has to learn that he cannot treat people like that. You, me or anyone. Ever, you understand? Because you need to realise that too.'

'Don't you fucking patronise me!' she screamed, running past me to pick up Roman. Now he did wake, with a start. God help the poor tot. 'This is my baby, you understand me? My baby, so just butt OUT!'

She hauled him up and flew from the room, the blanket trailing behind her.

I sat down then and gave up with thinking how best to proceed. I was shot, and needed Mike home to help us find a way forward. Till then I just cried. Cried very hard.

Chapter 16

I had probably been too optimistic, that was the crux of it. Too *ideal*istic, as well. What had happened – well, how earth-shattering a development was it really? Underage mum, difficult background, boyfriend known to social services ... Throw in a bit of sexual jealousy, some mischief-making – for goodness only knew what juvenile reason – and you had the recipe for what happened next right there. Which was just so depressing, and it gnawed at me with a furious insistence. And more than that, with a sense that I should have expected it to happen. Which in turn made me cross with my cynical alter ego – what was so wrong with hoping for the best outcome, anyway?

But for all that I'd pinned my hopes on Tarim getting his act together, what were the chances of that happening in reality? That was Mike's take on things when he got back and got his update, and the rest of the weekend played slowly out.

Emma barely spoke to me, except in sullen monosyllables, and I despaired of finding a way to get her to understand that her loyalty to Tarim was so misplaced. But I knew I must. I had seen enough to absorb the whole chilling picture. There were clearly two sides to Tarim and, dispiriting though it was to think it, where Emma was concerned, anyway, there probably always would be, too.

It was Monday now – a drizzly day to match the prevailing mood – and I was just wiping mushy rusks from Roman's chubby cheeks when the doorbell rang. I knew who it would be – Hannah and Maggie. After I made the call to John he'd filled both women in, and this morning's meeting had been convened as a matter of priority. The plan was that they'd come out to give Emma a 'wake-up call'. Whatever that was. I still wasn't clear what would actually happen now. And Emma didn't even seem to care. When I'd explained to her on the previous afternoon that they were coming over for a chat with her, her only comment had been a sour-faced 'whatever'.

Popping Roman down in his playpen – Emma was still upstairs, showering – I had a glance round to check the house was at least reasonably presentable, then went out into the hall to let them in. I opened the door to find two faces professionally arranged into 'now it's time we got serious about things' masks.

Which was fine – they were right. Getting serious was what was needed here. But at the same time I felt a slight frisson of defensiveness on seeing them, as if, while my head said we were batting for the same 'welfare of the child' team, my heart was resisting the idea.

I pushed it aside as I led them both into the sitting room, and Roman, as if schooled by a drama coach, pulled himself up onto his legs and grinned and bounced excitedly as the two of them went over the better to fawn at him.

'Oh, he's just adorable!' Hannah cooed as she smoothed her hand over his inky curls. She turned then. 'You're doing a great job with him, Casey.'

'Me?' I shook my head. 'Well, yes, I do play a part obviously, but, you know, despite her – ahem – poor choices when it comes to boyfriends, Emma's actually turning into a lovely little mum.'

It had come out unthinkingly, but seeing the look Hannah and Maggie had exchanged when I'd spoken made me feel suddenly wary. 'She is,' I persisted. 'You should see the two of them together. She dotes on him, she really does. You must have seen for yourself, Hannah …' There was no response, other than another surreptitious look passed between them. I felt my stomach plummet to my toes. 'Anyway,' I finished lamely, 'who's for coffee?'

I had thought that it would be best if I stayed out of the way while Hannah and Maggie spoke to Emma, so, after calling her down and then delivering coffee and biscuits, I went to take Roman out of the room and leave them to it.

'No, no, stay, Casey,' Maggie urged. 'This obviously concerns you as well.'

So I stayed, entertaining Roman while the two of them berated Emma, telling her how irresponsible she'd been and how much she'd let them down. They also told her that what had happened between her and Tarim – both the violence and the drunken visitation – had set things way back in terms of them trusting him with Roman. Emma had remained silent throughout but now looked directly at Hannah.

'With Roman? What's that supposed to mean? That was nothing to do with Roman.'

Maggie patiently explained that, because of the aggression Tarim had shown towards Emma, contact would continue to remain supervised for the foreseeable future and she wouldn't be allowed to go to either Tarim or his dad's house with the baby for at least the next few weeks.

'It all depends on Tarim,' she finished, 'as I'm sure you can appreciate, Emma. He'll be starting from scratch again, given the way he's behaved. And he won't be getting any further chances.'

Emma's mouth had been set in a thin line as she listened to this. 'You can't fucking do that,' she said now, making me wince. 'You can't make promises and then break them whenever you feel like it! This is you lot all over, this is – you make your fucking rules up as you go along! Great,' she said, 'this is just fucking great!'

'Emma,' I began, anxious to at least bring the bad language under control. But Hannah spoke over me.

'Emma,' she said sharply, 'are you aware that your baby is right here, in his playpen, and that you're shouting and swearing in front of him?'

Emma looked at her witheringly. 'He's eight months, not eight years. I'm not an idiot! He doesn't understand.'

'He can hear your tone of voice, though,' Hannah persisted. 'And it's upsetting him. Can't you see that?' She was right. Roman was indeed looking anxiously at his mum now. I resisted the urge to pick him up, and instead let Hannah press her point home. 'And getting back to what you said, actually, we can change the rules, Emma. We can change them whenever we feel we need to, to protect Roman. I'm sorry, but you and Tarim have brought this on yourselves. You are lucky to have Mike and Casey fighting your corner for you, actually, because believe me, in other circumstances, you might have lost more than you bargained for.'

There was a silence then, as we all took this in. Then Emma spoke. She was shaking and I could see tears pooling in her eyes. 'Well, fuck you!' she shouted. 'Fuck you!'

Maggie flinched, Hannah looked stony and now Roman responded, bursting into the sort of wail that meant I could no longer ignore him. And since I was closest, I plucked him from his play pen.

'You see?' Hannah said, her patience by now clearly frazzled. 'Is this what you want for your child? To feel constantly anxious and upset like this? To see his mummy swearing, and with her face black and blue, and letting the man who did it get away with it? Do you think that's fair on him? Do you think that's what he wants? To be so scared? To feel you care more for some low-life boyfriend than your own little boy's welfare?'

The words had come out, I could see, without Hannah really thinking. And she meant well. She just wanted to make Emma *see*. So I felt a little sorry for her as Emma squared up to her, finger raised and trembling. Glancing at me, as if to acknowledge that she really needed to do this, she scowled at the startled twenty-something in disgust. If looks could have killed, she would have floored her, for sure.

'You really *don't* have a clue, do you? Welcome to *my* world,' she said.

For a time after the meeting, I felt hopeful for progress. After the two social workers had gone – Emma had already fled the room, distraught, by then – I had put Roman down for his nap on a makeshift bed within the playpen and gone upstairs to see how she was doing.

And she was crying, curled up foetally, clutching a pillow to her chest and weeping into it. And I knew why, too. She was crying for the childhood she'd never had. For the mother who had always put her men before her little one. Had put the drugs and the alcohol before her too. Oh, it wasn't that simple – I knew that – these things were always complicated. There was no simple 'bad person' tag you could affix. Who knew what demons caused Emma's mum to fail Emma so badly? Who knew what injustices and cruelties had been visited on her?

But for a child there is no room for excuses, justifications. The best that could be hoped for, long term, was that, at some point in adulthood, she would come to understand why her mum had failed her and learn to deal with it.

And I knew why she was so upset, hearing those few words from Hannah – it was because, despite her attitude, she desperately didn't want to repeat the cycle with Roman. She wanted the best for him. I truly believed that.

I sat down on the bed and stroked her back, and she seemed happy enough to let me. And after a time the crying quietened and she lowered the pillow enough to speak.

'I fucked up again, didn't I?' she said quietly, wiping her good eye with a corner of the pillowcase. The swollen one I noticed she left well alone, so it was obviously still sore, even if less swollen. 'I've just made everything worse for us now, haven't I?' she finished. 'I just get so angry with them. They just don't understand.'

I told her everything would work out, that all she had to do was keep doing what she was doing with Roman and prove to social services she was a good, responsible mother. I told her that she was a good mum – anyone could see how much she loved Roman. It was just that Hannah and Maggie had to know she was prepared to put him first – and that Tarim understood that if he wanted to play a role then he had to grow up, mend his ways and show he cared for them.

Emma sat up. 'Casey,' she said. 'Would you speak to him, please? He wanted to call you, but I told him best not till I'd asked you. He's just, like, *so* sorry. He's been crying and everything – he *knows* he did wrong. An' he'll do whatever it takes – you know, the family centre and shit, basically – like, everything it takes. He's so sorry. He just lost it, and he knows he did and he wants to put things right again. Casey, he's not like you think he is. He really *isn't*.'

I patted her. This was not the time to dredge the whole thing up again, even if the image of Tarim crying – hot, self-pitying tears, I didn't doubt – stuck in my craw. 'I know,' I soothed, 'I know. Let's just give it a couple of weeks, eh?' I smoothed a finger across her brow, just above her swollen eye socket. 'If I speak to him now I might feel much too inclined to give him a piece of my mind, Emma. No, let's leave it a couple of weeks. Let everything calm down. Let him *show* that he means it as well as tell us he does, eh?' I smiled. 'And I'm not talking flowers here, okay?'

A week passed. Ten days. A run of blistering ones. There was one meeting with Tarim at the same family centre, and though all I saw of him was a glimpse when we picked up Emma and Roman he was at pains to wave manically as we left. He clearly wanted us to like him – to accept him and forgive him – and, in that sense, I did believe his feelings for Emma were genuine. It was just the small matter of leopards and spots. The world was full of men who loved their women to distraction; trouble was that a few of them also saw their women as possessions and, if challenged, saw physical aggression as their right. Was he one such? I really wished I didn't think so.

In the short term, however, I had a new period to look forward to. It was almost the start of the school summer holidays, which meant no school for Emma and much less baby minding for me, which I didn't feel disloyal for telling Riley I really welcomed; treasure though Roman was, looking after babies all day was time-consuming. And also limiting – when you had to have a baby in tow at all times, there were lots of small freedoms that had to be curtailed.

No, I was looking forward to being able to spend much more quality time with my grandsons, not to mention my pregnant daughter, and the rest of the family too. I was also pleased that there would be lots of opportunities to do some fun things with the little ones, which would very much include Emma and little Roman.

I was just thinking this, while peeling potatoes for chips, when I heard my mobile chirrup in my bag. It was just after three, which meant Emma should be home within the hour. It was the last day of term, though, so perhaps she'd stay on a bit – bond with her friends, perhaps make plans for some outings.

I quickly wiped my hands and grabbed the phone from the pocket. It was Tash, I could see – Emma's friend.

'Casey?' she said, and I could tell right away that there was something to be concerned about in her voice.

'Tash?' I said. 'What is it? Are you at school?'

'We didn't go in,' she said. 'We – um – well, a few of us didn't, actually. It was, like the last day, an' – well, we went to this flat, an' well, she got pissed and – I don't think she *meant* to, but – oh, Casey, I'm –'

She was stumbling over her words. She was clearly worse for wear herself. 'Tash,' I said, 'where are you? Where is Emma?'

'I'm at the hospital –' she started.

'*Hospital?*'

'Casey, I *know* she didn't mean to. She'd just had all this cider. And then some shots, and – then, well, she had like this *massive* row with Taz then, and –'

'Tarim? Tarim was there?' Visions of further violence flooded my brain now.

'No, no,' Tash reassured me. So that was something to be grateful for. 'It was on the phone,' she went on, 'but, like, really, really bad. I think he dumped her. An' she was like "I'll show him", and so in the end we called an ambulance and –'

'Show him by doing what, Tash?'

'She took some pills, so –'

'Oh my God. Look love, I need to get down there to you, don't I? The general hospital? Right. I'm on my way.'

I ended the call and tried to get my head together. I couldn't believe it. Couldn't believe she would do this again – what about Roman? Shit, I thought. What *about* Roman?

I grabbed my phone again, pressed some buttons and connected with Riley, who was thankfully in. That done – and thank goodness, she was round to me in minutes – I hot-footed it over to the hospital.

On the way there I felt uncharacteristically frightened. I was a born optimist, hard-wired to look on the bright side, but right now I couldn't seem to grab a single positive thought. They were all crowded out by so many negatives.

Chief among them, of course, was the daddy of all the bad ones I could imagine – that Emma would this time have succeeded where last time she failed.

It was a chilling thought. She'd been drunk, perhaps very drunk – Tash had mentioned shots – and kids regularly managed to kill themselves with drugs and alcohol without even trying, didn't they? And if you took that in tandem with another row with Tarim … I gripped the steering wheel and willed the car to eat the miles up faster. It hardly bore thinking about.

So when I got to the hospital and was taken through it was with a massive surge of relief that I heard the brisk but kindly nurse say the words I most needed to hear, namely, 'She's fine.'

'What a silly girl, though,' she added, once she'd established I was Emma's foster mum, 'because, of course, she was in such a to-do about the idea of us pumping out her stomach, so it's just a blessing she'd got so inebriated that she sicked the whole lot up again. And that, thankfully, there weren't really very many pills in her, because otherwise we would have had to insist. Boyfriend blues, I hear,' she added, her matter-of-fact manner acting like balm on my emotionally frazzled mindset. But then she sighed. 'Seriously though, Mrs Watson, I don't mind telling you we've had *very* stern words with her. Easy to blame the hormones, I suppose, but you'll perhaps want to keep an eye on her. An extremely silly thing to do at any time – especially for a not-quite fifteen-year-old – but a particularly stupid thing to do when pregnant. This could have had a *very* different outcome, as I'm sure you're all too aware.'

I did a double take. Had she really just said the word *pregnant*?

'Did you just –' I began.

She blinked at me. 'You mean you didn't *know* she was pregnant?'

I shook my head.

'No,' I confessed, 'I didn't.'

She returned my look of shock with a 'been there and done that' expression.

'Ah,' she said, 'and, well – now you do know – yes, she is. Around ten weeks or so, she reckons, give or take.' She gestured to the furthest of a row of A&E cubicles. 'I think you'd better go and have a chat with her, don't you?'

My mind was a blur of a different kind as I walked the dozen or so feet to the cubicle. When had this happened, then? I counted back. Must have been immediately Tarim was released from jail, must have been. Which seemed logical. Oh, the stupid, stupid girl – how could she have been so reckless? And stupid me, for not having a conversation with her about contraception at any point either. I could have kicked myself, much good *that* would do now. And then another thought zoomed up and slapped me round the face for good measure. Was that what those rows had been about? Did Tarim already know she was pregnant? Did he do the maths and work out that it couldn't have been his? I wished I had a calendar. It was tight – it was conceivable that it *could* have been someone else's. What a mess.

And more to the point, what would happen now?

Chapter 17

Emma had her back to me when I entered, lying curled up on her side, presumably sleeping. Tash was sitting in a chair, glued to her mobile. She was massively pregnant herself now and I felt a rush of both sympathy and gratitude. This was the last thing she needed to be dealing with.

She hauled herself to her feet as I parted the curtain. 'Oh, you're here,' she said. 'Great. I've got to get back or I'll get into trouble.'

I didn't comment that I imagined she was probably in trouble anyway, what with bunking off school and going to some lad's flat. But they would go easy on her, I was sure, given her condition.

'How will you get home?' I asked her, shrugging off my jacket. The place was roasting. 'Are you going to be okay? You look like you're due any day.'

She waggled her phone at me. 'I've sorted a lift, thanks. I just texted my mate. He's going to come and get me now.'

Then she turned to Emma. 'You okay, babes? Text me, then, yeah?'

I saw Emma nod slightly, so she obviously wasn't asleep, just weak and sick and resting her eyes. As I came round the side of the bed I noticed there was a small cardboard bowl by her pillow. She looked impossibly tiny. Frighteningly young.

'Well, thanks for having the presence of mind to call an ambulance, Tash,' I said. I smiled at her. 'You did well. You did brilliantly. Emma's lucky to have such a wonderful friend.'

At which Tash blushed to the roots of her hair, bless her.

Emma rolled onto her back and groaned as soon as Tash left us. And almost immediately sat up instead, retching. I grabbed the bowl and passed it to her, then scooped her hair up and held it, while she threw up a cupful of what mostly looked like water.

She sat back again, spent, looking a fetching shade of green. 'I've really done it this time, haven't I, Casey?'

I reached for the jug beside her and poured her half a glass of water. 'Just sips,' I said. 'Don't gulp it or you'll set your stomach off again.' Then I pulled the chair closer and sat on it. 'So,' I said, 'how long have you known?'

She sniffed. 'That I was pregnant? Pretty much since I missed the first period. And then when I didn't come on again.' She groaned. 'God, I feel so *ill*.'

'So you told the nurse …'

'I thought I'd better. In case, you know – because of the pills and that and everything. And if they wanted to pump my stomach …'

Which wouldn't have mattered, I knew that much, but there was no point in telling Emma that. In fact, her thinking it might had been a blessing, in some ways. Had she not been worried, when *would* I have known? Not till it was too late to do anything about it? 'And it's definitely Tarim's?' I asked.

She looked aghast. 'Of *course* it's Tarim's – who else's would it be?'

'Love, after the things you've been saying to me – and that shiner he gave you … Not to mention his mad drunken rant outside our house – well, you can't blame me for asking the question, can you?'

Emma shook her head. Her hair looked like strands of oily spaghetti, and her clothes – a grimy T-shirt and pastel skinny jeans – looked like they'd been dunked in the pasta water, too. What the hell had she been doing all day? And with her pregnant, as well. Drowning her sorrows? I decided this wasn't the time to ask her about the latest spat with Tarim. There was a bigger thing at stake now – a potentially equally grim situation. She was a few weeks shy of fifteen, that was all. Still a child. She'd have two kids before she hit sixteen – it was unthinkable.

'Love,' I said quietly, 'have you thought about what you're going to do now? I mean, you don't have to have another baby – you know that, don't you?'

Emma turned towards me, her expression one of shock.

'I'm not getting rid of it,' she said. 'I don't believe in abortions. I'm keeping it.'

I opened my mouth to speak and then shut it again, quickly. Much as my knee-jerk reaction was to start up a dialogue to try and convince her otherwise, it wasn't my place to. Or my professional remit. I had no right. Young as she was, it was her body, her baby, her absolute right to choose, and it wouldn't be me who tried to interfere with that. If other people – other professionals – wanted to say something about it, then well and good. But it wouldn't be me who'd be imposing any belief system on her. There was an option and I had mentioned it, as was my duty. But there it stopped. What happened now was out of my hands.

They decided to keep Emma in overnight. So I travelled home alone, to find a concerned Mike and Riley at home waiting for me, anxious for more detail than that which I'd already texted, the gist of which was just *on way back now*, *Emma recovering*, *but also pregnant*, followed up with a sincerely felt *arrgghh!*

Not that any of us felt the breeziness the exclamation points might have suggested.

'How on earth will she cope, mum?' Riley wanted to know, shaking her head. 'She struggles to cope with the responsibility of looking after one baby, so how the hell is she ever going to manage two?'

'Especially with that waste of space for a boyfriend,' Mike added. And he wasn't even up to speed with the latest development. He might have an even stronger description in mind once he was. Though, if it was true that Tarim had dumped her, so much the better for her, as far as I was concerned.

I shook my head. 'I don't think it will come to that now, do you?'

'What?' said Mike. 'Is she talking about having a termination or something?'

'Not at all,' I said, sitting down wearily. 'Quite the opposite. She says there's no way she's doing that and I'm pretty sure she won't be shifted. But think about it.' I raised a finger and thumb and held the tips together. 'Social services are *this* close to taking Roman out of her care, I'm sure of it. And with all that's happened – bloody overdoses, domestic violence, another pregnancy … I think we have to face it. It's odds on they're going to put him into care now.'

'But he's *already* in care, Mum,' Riley pointed out. '*You're* his carers! Don't say that. Don't say they'd do that – surely they'd let us keep him, wouldn't they? Just transfer him over to you officially – wouldn't that be how they'd work it? Just change it so that it's you, and not Emma, who's in charge of him.'

I shrugged. 'I suppose they might, but I can't quite see it. Can you, Mike? After all, we're talking a whole different situation than the one we have with Emma. He's a baby, remember – which means we really are talking long term. Who knows how long?'

We all fell silent, as we each contemplated the possible scenarios. None of which, frankly, I wanted. Oh,

God, I thought, trying to imagine being Emma. Imagine the thought of that happening – 'Sorry, love, but we're taking your baby from you. That's it. You failed. Say goodbye.'

I couldn't begin to imagine where you'd start telling a girl that was going to happen. Whatever she'd said before about losing him and just 'trying for another one' I knew losing Roman would break Emma's heart. And, thinking that, I realised something else, with a start: that this was the first time I'd properly addressed the possibility of giving Roman up myself. And it upset me. Upset me even more than I'd ever thought it would. And I knew why, too. Because all along I'd had this private sense of certainty that when Emma left us they would still have that connection with the family. That she'd stay in touch, that perhaps we'd see him – at the very least know how he was doing. Still feel connected to him. This was different. This was facing the very real possibility that Hannah would come and pick him up one day, we'd say our goodbyes, and that would be that; we'd never see him again.

It made me want to burst into tears. I cleared my throat. 'Let's not pre-judge,' I said. 'Let's wait and see what happens. They know we'd be happy to keep him, and more importantly we're also now cleared for babies. Which means … No, let's wait. Let's just wait and see.'

We didn't have to wait very long. The very next day, before we'd even gone to collect Emma from hospital, Maggie was on the phone saying they'd made their decision. With the events of recent weeks, and in particular the events of yesterday, they had no choice. They were indeed taking Roman into care.

'So we'll come round to explain things later this afternoon, if that's okay? Will you have got her home by then, do you think?'

I told her I would. 'But, listen,' I said. 'Mike and I have been talking about this possibility arising and, you know, we really would like to foster him ourselves – honestly, Maggie, we'd be happy to. He's settled here, he knows us, he has his routines and everything …'

Her voice cut across me like a gust of freezing air. 'I don't think that's possible,' she said. 'In fact, I know it isn't, because we've already discussed it. We feel it's in Roman's best interests if we remove him from Emma completely, and as you're fostering Emma we can't achieve that if we entrust him to you, can we?' She sighed. 'Look, I know you don't want to hear it, Casey, but I'm afraid we don't see this as a short-term arrangement – not a temporary thing … look, I'm sorry to cut you short, but I have to go into a meeting now. Have a chat with John, why don't you? He's up to speed with things. I'm sure he'd be happy to answer your questions …'

I gripped the chair back as I disconnected, thinking I was going to have a panic attack or something. My questions? Answer my *questions*? I could hardly catch my breath, let alone formulate questions, like this was some sort of administrative issue. What about feelings in all this? What about hearts?

A Last Kiss for Mommy

I looked across at Roman, obliviously playing with his plastic bricks on the floor, and in that instant I knew I'd made the worst mistake ever in allowing this beautiful little boy to come into my life. I should have heeded Mike, should have heeded that inner voice that was so insistent. *You'll get too involved*, it had kept saying to me. *Don't do it. You'll get way too emotionally involved*. And then have my heart broken. It was breaking now, as I watched him crawl excitedly towards me, with his chubby cheeks and his two front teeth and his powerful little fingers, clutching at the fabric of my jeans, gripping as he hauled himself up.

'Meemaw,' he was saying to me, grinning. 'Meemaw! Meemaw!' I scooped him up and held him close to me, my tears wetting his face. 'Oh, baby,' I said, 'I'm so sorry. I'm so, so sorry.'

I was crying when I phoned Mike and asked him if he could come home for a bit, and still crying when he phoned John Fulshaw – I simply couldn't face it – and asked him if it was possible for Maggie or Hannah to go and pick Emma up tomorrow instead, because I simply couldn't face doing any more of this on my own. They spoke for what seemed like ages, and I didn't like the sound of any of it. And I'd been right.

'It's pretty straightforward, love,' Mike said finally. 'I'm sorry. As we've committed to keeping Emma then Roman really *does* have to go elsewhere. Clean break.'

'Clean break?' I sobbed. 'There's nothing "clean" about any of this!'

'Love,' he said softly, 'they've already got a placement in mind for him. I get the feeling this was already done and dusted a couple of weeks ago. That they were just hanging on for the inevitable.'

'Exactly. Just waiting for her to fail!'

Mike sat down beside me on the sofa. Roman was flat out asleep now, at the other end of it, one foot sticking out from the little cot blanket. 'No, love, not that,' Mike said. 'Waiting and hoping that it didn't have to come to that. Look, the bottom line is that we can choose if we want to. John didn't say so in so many words. But the truth is that we can keep one of them – just not both of them. One or the other. If we weren't committed to Emma then of course we'd be in with a shout at fostering Roman, but, as John said, it never came up, because they knew we wouldn't do that.'

For a split second my brain went into a fast and furious overdrive. What if we did just that? Gave Emma up and concentrated our efforts on little Roman? And for a split second the idea felt so seductive. Swap this difficult teenager who wouldn't listen to me, who couldn't – wouldn't – see reason. And particularly in relation to Tarim. This teenager who pigheadedly refused to listen to *any* of the advice I gave her, who let me down, abused my trust and gave me grief at every turn.

But even as the thoughts rose in my mind, the bile rose alongside them. What was *I thinking*? That wasn't me. That wasn't what I was here for. It was precisely for the reasons I'd just grabbed at to try and justify my selfish thinking that Emma needed me – needed all of us – so much more.

A zillion times more. She was damaged and she was hurting, and she'd already been rejected. What had I been *thinking*? It was utterly insane. That beautiful baby would most likely settle anywhere. Settle, and be happy, and forget. He would have no memory of the first complicated year of his life, and that would be a blessing. He might wonder later where he came from, try to establish his family tree. But having been so small, he would not remember any of it. And without memories to haunt him, he would not hurt. Not so much. Not in the way his poor, poor mother would, anyway.

No, we were committed, and we were right to be committed. Emma needed us. There was no going back now.

It was done swiftly and brutally, but then, was there any other way? No one meant to be brutal. They were just saying words. But Emma's howl, as she sank to her knees in the middle of the living room, was like that of a mortally wounded animal. 'Oh, please, no,' she pleaded. 'Oh, please, please don't do this. I'm begging you, please don't take my baby from me!'

'I'm so sorry, Emma,' Maggie said, 'but it's out of our hands now. And he's going to the loveliest couple, who will take such good care of him, I promise. And you can have contact, once it's all sorted out, at the family centre, just like before, and you can take photographs, and so can they,

and pass on letters and pictures and little presents and so
on –'

But I could see that every word she said in an effort to
make things better was just making it so, so much worse.
'Please,' Emma begged, '*please*. I'll be a good mum, I promise. Casey, *tell* them – tell them what a good mum I am,
please!' She was on all fours now, rocking slightly, and
clutching at my leg. I sank down next to her and pulled her
close to me, feeling the thump of her heart in her skinny
ribcage. I was crying too now. I didn't have a clue what to
say.

'I'm sorry,' was all I could manage. 'I'm so sorry, sweetie,
I really am. We'll get through this, we'll sort out contact,
we'll make it regular – and as soon as possible …'

Emma pushed me away then, though not roughly; just
with a definite sense of purpose. Wiping her eyes on her
sleeve she walked in a determined manner into the dining
room, where Roman was sleeping in his buggy. Or rather
had been. He was awake now and waving his arms at her.

'When?' she said, turning around. 'When are you taking
him?'

I looked at Maggie, wondering. A couple of weeks,
perhaps? I hoped so. Give us time. Time with Roman, time
to get everything sorted. Time, perhaps, for Emma to
choose a couple of nice things to send with him. She'd
always cared so much that he looked nice, after all.

'Tomorrow,' Maggie said. 'I'll come back around 9 a.m.'

'Tomorrow?' I gaped. I could see the colour drain from
Emma's face. I stood up, and so did Mike – I think we both

thought she might faint – but she only swayed and, looking at Roman, seemed to be torn about what to do. For a moment I thought she might actually snatch him up and make a run for it. But she didn't. She simply touched his nose tenderly with her finger, than rushed past us both and out of the room.

'I'm so sorry,' Maggie said to Mike and me as the air in the room resettled. 'I know this must be difficult. I know how much you have obviously all bonded with little Roman.'

'Difficult?' Mike gaped at her. 'Difficult? You have no idea. This whole thing is just awful. We're all in bits about it – Casey in particular. And we can't even *begin* to imagine what's going on in that poor girl's head up there.'

He came across to me and put his arm around my shoulder. He squeezed it hard, and I tried equally hard not to start sobbing again all over him. It would just be so unseemly in such a measured, professional, even clinical sort of gathering. Which was exactly how it felt to me – clinical.

Mike obviously thought so too. 'Look, I'm sorry,' he said to the two women perched so incongruously on our sofa. 'If there's nothing else, I think we'd like to be left alone for a bit. First thing in the morning, you say? Well, we'll have him all ready for when you get here. No point in prolonging the agony, is there?' He sniffed. 'If there's paperwork to sort, then that's fine, just let us know what you need later – email it through. Whatever. And we'll make sure you have it ready for when you get here.'

Hannah stood up and smoothed her top down, closely followed by Maggie. 'Would you like me to pop up and have another word with Emma before we go?' Hannah asked me. 'You know, just to make sure she's okay?'

Mike shook his head stiffly. 'Thanks, but I don't think so.'

'Right, then,' said Maggie as we showed them out. 'See you both in the morning, then. And once again, we're sorry.'

Well, what else *could* they say?

Chapter 18

The day they took Roman away will remain etched in my memory for ever. Of all the difficult days I have ever experienced as a foster carer, saying goodbye to that little boy was one of the most traumatic. The whole family had come round to say farewell to him and support us. Mostly to support Emma, of course, because this was a terrible, terrible thing to happen in such a young life, and I already feared for the effect it might have on her. But also to support me, because I was an emotional wreck.

And I wasn't the only one. Poor Kieron was so traumatised he couldn't even bear to be a part of it, and when Maggie arrived he took himself off out into the back garden with his dog, Bob, both because he didn't want anyone to catch him crying – which he was – but also because he just couldn't cope. And I was so moved. Yes, I knew a part of it was related to his Asperger's (he hated change) but it was also because, though Kieron hadn't lived with Roman himself, Roman had become part of the family, just like all the other children who had passed through our lives – part of the 'furniture', part of the regular routine of Kieron and Lauren coming round to see us. As the song goes – he'd become accustomed to Roman's face.

Riley and David had come round too and, bless her, my daughter understood. While David herded the boys into some semblance of order, she stayed close beside me, almost as if gently reminding me that there was new and greater happiness just around the corner, in the form of that new granddaughter that was on the way.

Right then, however, I was finding it difficult to keep it together. Who would have thought this would feel so much like a bereavement? Silly, because that's exactly the conversation we'd had at the outset – that I would fall in love with this baby (I always fell in love with babies) and be desolate on the day he finally left us.

Maggie was quick and efficient. Recruiting David and little Levi, with Jackson clamouring to carry something too, she soon had all the belongings Roman would be taking with him in the car, and was passing Roman himself round for last hugs and kisses. I did mine quickly. I just couldn't stand to prolong the pain further.

In the midst of all this was Emma, who'd dressed Roman in his newest favourite outfit: a pair of distressed jeans and sailor-style hoody that said 'Captain', topped off by the coolest little herringbone flat cap. And as I watched her bewildered face, amid all the bustle and activity, I tried to remember the last time I'd felt such a dull, heavy and all-embracing ache. And it truly all but finished me off when she finally took him from Maggie, hefting him high in her arms just to bring about that familiar chuckle, then crushing him tightly to her chest. 'Come on, darling,' she whispered, 'just one last kiss for Mummy.' It was so quiet then that you could hear every syllable.

I couldn't bear to wave him off, so, though I knew my place was really beside Emma, I chickened out, and let Riley step in and console her. I needed to escape for a few minutes, so while everyone gathered on the doorstep I fled into the garden to be with Kieron. I shouldn't have really, because – there was one thing that upset Kieron that *was* under my control, and that was him seeing *me* upset.

He took one look at me and I could see his features changing and crumpling. 'Why do you still do this, Mum?' he wanted to know. 'How can you stand it? I don't think I can cope with it again.'

I threw my arms around him, all six foot three of masculine angles and reassuring bulk, and felt moved beyond words at the simplicity of his logic. Why would you do something that made you periodically feel so empty? So sad? To Kieron's mind, that made no sense.

'You will cope, we all will. We'll start to feel better. It's part of the job. You know that saying? You have to be brave to love? Well, it's true. It's not for the fainthearted because it *does* hurt when things like this happen. But there's a balance, and on balance it's a job that makes me happy. Makes us all happy in our own way, don't you think?'

Kieron nodded, though I could see he still wasn't convinced.

'And there's another thing,' I said. 'We've got to remember Emma. It's sad for us, but we've got to remember that Roman isn't ours. It felt like he belonged to us, but, actually, he didn't. He's Emma's and we have to be strong for her now. Hey,' I said, 'just think, if we feel like this, just imagine how *she* must be feeling.'

Kieron snorted bitterly. 'It's her fault, Mum! She could have done the right thing. But she didn't and I'll never forgive her for that.'

I was glad we were in the garden, well out of earshot of anyone. Kieron dealt in absolutes and right then that was how he felt, I knew.

I shook my head. 'It's not her fault, babes. She has lots and lots of problems. The odds were stacked against her from the start. What with her mother, and then Tarim, and look where she is now? Back in a bad place and it's up to us to support her. We can't turn away from her now, love. We have to help make sure she gets it right this time. Or else what's the point? We *have* to help her.'

It was to prove easier said than done. Forget the histrionics and the 'cry for help' 'overdoses', now it seemed Emma really had lost the will to live. It was a good thing school had broken up, because it was all she could do to get out of bed at some point during the day, though at the same time the lack of a routine wasn't helping – it would have been better if there had been something to distract her.

Other than Tarim, that was. He was still on the scene. Well, trying to be. But even Tarim couldn't divert Emma's attention from the pain she was so clearly feeling. They spoke often on the phone – I sometimes even heard them – but it seemed to be Tarim calling Emma, rather than Emma calling him, and on those occasions when I over-heard any of their conversations, they seemed short, blunt, directionless, pointless-seeming phone calls, and a part of me at least hoped that whatever feelings she'd had for him would soon be extinguished – as they must surely be as the reality of what had happened began to sink in, including how much his behaviour had brought it about.

Tash was wonderful and even though she was a brand new mum herself now – she, too, had had a baby boy – she still stopped by frequently in the days that followed, leaving her baby with her auntie, and seemed dauntless in the face of Emma's lassitude. She was a great girl, so giving, and I hoped their relationship would deepen; she had a maturity about her and a spontaneous warmth – whatever the details of her own difficult upbringing, someone along the way had clearly done something right.

My main concern, however, was for Emma's health. She was carrying a new baby now, and with the weight drop-ping off her – weight she couldn't afford to lose in the first place – I began to fret about making sure she was fit enough. I tried to bring it up more than once, to gently encourage her to think about the new life inside her, but, perhaps understandably, it fell on deaf ears. For all her insistence that she didn't believe in terminations, it was as if the

human inside her – whose right to life she had so champi-
oned – was no longer of any consequence whatever.

And I could understand that, because she ached so much
for Roman. The silence was deafening, as was the absence
of baby mess, the absence of that distinctive baby smell. It
hurt me enough, so God only knew what it was doing to
Emma. It would be a physical, visceral pain. She had been
to see him once, and it had clearly been a traumatising
experience. She came back ashen and silent and would not
talk about it. So I didn't press her, realising it would do
more harm than good. She was depressed, plain and simple,
and, with medication a complete no-no, I knew time, and
the hope that she could one day have him back with her,
were the only routes that would help her find her way out.
I was all for keeping positive about the likelihood of the
latter, however doubtful Maggie and Hannah might be, but
time was something, in terms of the baby growing inside
her, that we didn't have an unending supply of. She needed
to think about the here and now, and get into pregnancy
mode. She needed to be seen by the local GP – our ever-
reliable Dr Shakelton – and have antenatal appointments
and scans arranged.

I gave it three weeks, then I knew I needed to put wheels
in motion, and when Riley was round one day with the
boys – we were going on a picnic – I had a brainwave. 'You
know, I've been thinking,' I told her. 'You two must be the
same amount gone, give or take. Do you think – assuming
you're willing – that we might be able to organise it so she
can go for hers with you?'

Riley laughed. She had been such a tonic since Roman had left us. It was such a comfort to know she knew how I felt. 'You mean "be dragged along with me, kicking and screaming", don't you, Mum?'

'Well, kind of.' I smiled ruefully. She'd hit the nail on the head there. In her current state, left to her own devices, Emma would be giving birth behind a bush. 'I just think it would help her to focus,' I said. 'Have some of your enthusiasm and energy rub off on her, too.'

'Energy?' Riley scoffed. 'I'm not so sure about the energy bit, given that I now have a whole summer ahead running around after the boys. I'll be nodding off on her shoulder, no doubt.'

It seemed such a simple plan that I knew, due to sod's law, that there would be some reason it wouldn't happen, but Riley didn't see why it couldn't. 'And you're right. It *will* be good for her,' she mused. 'And nice for me as well. Someone to keep me company during those long tedious hours in the waiting room, with nothing but a sugar-coated "what to expect" video running on a sick-making loop.'

She was lying, of course. Riley was a very social animal. She would probably pitch up in the antenatal clinic at 2 p.m. and by 5 have made three brand-new friends. So I was particularly touched that she was enthused by my idea. She'd made a good choice when she'd decided to go into fostering. She had the biggest heart imaginable, and I loved her for it.

* * *

And she was as good as her word. Over the next few weeks it was as if she had quietly appointed herself as Emma's guardian angel. It was a huge relief and I was so grateful. David was his usual reliable self, looking after the boys more than usual – quite often when he was knackered after a long, long day working – just so Riley could linger at ours and bond with Emma. And, slowly, it seemed to be working. Riley was just such a good counsellor, alternately pretending not to notice Emma's long face and lack of interest – jabbering on endlessly about baby things and new pregnancy tips and any other trivia that popped into her head – and then sometimes, with her acuity, sensing the time was right for it, gently coaxing Emma to open up more. Best of all she listened. She never tried to foist opinions or offer solutions. She just listened. I couldn't have been more proud of her.

And it seemed their blossoming relationship was helping in one particularly important way: helping Emma work through her feelings about Tarim. It was almost teatime one afternoon and I was in the kitchen, peeling potatoes, and the girls were sitting half-watching a music channel on TV while Levi and Jackson were kicking a ball around in the garden.

My children seem to think I share their taste in popular music. I don't, but I like to humour them so I still smiled and nodded when Riley popped her head in to tell me she'd leave the door open so I could hear too and wouldn't feel left out. Yes, it was a bit drony, but I didn't much mind – like any mum or gran, I guess, even if I was getting on with something else, I liked the background hum of family being around.

It also meant I could hear the pair of them chatting, and on this occasion my ears immediately pricked up. I don't know what had prompted it but I realised they were talking about the day Emma had bunked off and taken those pills.

'What made you do it, Ems?' I could hear Riley asking. 'You know, what actually triggered it? Something he said?'

'It was *insane*,' she said with feeling. 'It's like a blur now, the whole thing. I'd got so drunk – you know what it's like. Someone's like "Down it! Down it!" and you do –' There was a pause and I could imagine Riley nodding sagely, picturing this. 'And I just got it in my head to phone him – I don't know what for. It was the stupidest thing to do, ever – specially considering he knew I was pregnant. And he went mad about it – like he always did. He's such a piss-head' – she laughed – 'an' yet he always gives me so much grief about *me* drinking. And of course he did his usual thing of telling me he was on his way over and was going to kill me …'

'Kill you? A bit harsh …'

'Oh, that's what he always says. Thinks it makes him seem so hard – but it *so* doesn't. And of course I made the huge mistake of telling him not to bother doing that 'cos I was round Brett's house, and there were like half a dozen lads round, and that was it. And then the next thing is he's off on one about that boy I told you about – the one that fancied me? He's a mate of Brett's, of course, but there's never been *anything* going on, *ever* – and he's like, "Actually, you know what, slag, you can fuck off out of my life. Cos neither of your sprogs are mine, bottom line" – and then spouted all that DNA crap – and that's when it hit me. And I wanted to get him back, and I thought, sod it, I'll show you …' She tailed off then, and I could imagine Riley comforting her.

'And, like you say, Ems, you were pretty drunk.'

'Exactly.' I heard her sigh and sniff. 'God, I was *such* a twat.'

There was a pause. 'So, how about now?' Riley said eventually. 'Do you still think Taz loves you like he says he does?'

There was another pause. 'You know,' Emma said eventually, 'I just don't know. He says he does. Keeps calling. Sends me, like, a *zillion* texts a day. But it's like I only speak to him because I want to punish him – can you get that? I hate him. I think I hate him now. I know it sounds strange, but I almost wish he was still in prison. It was better then. When he was there for me, an' he loved me and that, but I could still have my own thoughts? Whenever he's around it's like I can't be me – like I'm on edge. Like I don't know what to think unless he tells me. It's like I'm actually better when he's *not* around. Does that sound completely mad?'

'Not at all,' I heard Riley saying. 'It makes a lot of sense.' She paused to speak to Levi who'd obviously come in and needed something. But then she went on. 'You know, the bottom line is that if you love someone, you love them, and that's fair enough, but if you want my opinion you can do much better than be with someone like him. Sure he says he loves you, but if he properly did, he'd love *you* – not some doormat who does everything he tells her. If he did, you'd feel yourself when you were with him, wouldn't you? Tell you what, Ems, you're so pretty and smart and strong, and being with someone like Tarim takes that away – it makes you weak.'

There was another long silence before Emma finally spoke. 'You know what,' she said. 'That's what Tash says. That's what everyone says. And it's like now I can think clearly and I can see why I lost Roman. Everything bad that's happened to me lately was either because of what Tarim's done to me or the way he's made me react.'

'Exactly,' said Riley. 'And you're stronger without him.'

'I know,' Emma said. 'That's what Tash and I've been saying. I think I'm better off being on my own for a while.'

The potatoes were done, the pan filled, the gas lit. In the middle of the kitchen I raised both arms towards the ceiling, then brought them down again, fist clenched. *Yes!* I mouthed. *Result!*

It turned out that they were both expecting girls. They'd both been keen to know, when they went for their eighteen-week scans – and went together, to the bemusement of the ultrasound operator. I went along too, of course, which caused some degree of consternation when we all piled in.

'Oh,' she said. 'You have two daughters expecting at the same time, I see. Two grandchildren all at once, eh? You'll have your hands full!'

We put her straight but, of course, she was absolutely right. There was a busy and emotionally intense time ahead. What I thought, but didn't say, though, was that I'd been thinking about that a lot. We'd committed to keeping Emma till she was sixteen – at least – but that had been before we'd known she was pregnant. It was something we'd need to discuss with John before too long, because if Emma wanted to try and get Roman back – which she did – then she would need to convince social services that she could function independently, as a single mum, living on her own.

But that was for the future. Right now, I was just happy to see both Riley and Emma smiling, as the paddle swept over the gel on their tummies in turn and the operator said, 'Yup, definitely a girl.'

Mike was over the moon, too, when I told him. As was Kieron. His principal concern, however, was that we mustn't be stereotypical – she must learn to love football just as much as her older brothers, and to that end he'd be buying her the same baby football strip that he'd got for both Levi and Jackson. Which made us all laugh out loud.

But if I'd thought everything was kind-of falling sort-of into place now, I was in for a nasty shock – we all were. And from a quarter that, preoccupied with the young girl in our care, I had never once imagined it might be coming. But just over a week later, at around 10 p.m., I took an unexpected call from Riley's David. He was so distraught he could hardly get the words out to explain. She'd had a miscarriage and had been rushed into hospital.

Chapter 19

Just as a pregnancy is an everyday miracle, so a miscarriage is an everyday tragedy. There was no rhyme or reason behind Riley losing her baby. It was just one of those things. Some glitch in the process. And though there had been blood tests and would be an investigation into all the whys and wherefores, the reality, as the doctor pointed out the next day, was that we'd probably never know.

Riley was crushed, just as any other mother to be would be, but also stoical. As she kept saying over and over, she had her boys, so she was one of the lucky ones, and the best thing she could do now was get over the physical upheaval, let her body heal and then get on with her life.

Emma – so young, so vulnerable, so understandably empathetic – was devastated too. When we told her the news the next morning, she was inconsolable. In an adult I might have been inclined to consider her distress self-indulgent, but she was just a child and had grown so close to Riley over recent weeks that I didn't doubt the sincerity of her feelings. She sat and sobbed for so long that she ended up puffy-eyed and exhausted, and once she'd stopped crying the smallest thing would set her off again, clutching her tiny bump and wailing till she had no tears left to shed.

I understood. I had a hunch these tears were partly for Roman, and perhaps cathartic – an opportunity to really express her sadness. Which, to some extent, I felt she'd really yet to do. Yes, she'd been low – her coming out of that was a joy for all to see – but at the same time the sense that she had brought it on herself complicated the business of grieving for her little boy. I felt strongly that she sensed she had no right to wallow in self-pity and that it had stopped her from forgiving herself.

In any event, a few days later she seemed transformed. We were well into the autumn term now, Levi and Jackson back in their usual school routine, and Emma too, albeit that it would be only temporary once again, was back in her unit, reconnecting with her education. I had obviously encouraged this, though not for the reasons usually given. Emma could finish her education at any point she chose to, truth be told – we now lived in a world where it was seen as a lifelong thing, learning – and I wasn't unduly worried that the best time might not be yet. What was more important, to my mind, was that she get back into a routine, just like the boys had – have a reason to get up in the mornings, go somewhere, have something to achieve every day and, most importantly, be among friends. She'd also mentioned that she quite liked the idea of eventually training to do hairdressing, reasoning (with exemplary logic, I thought) that it would work well with children, as she could become a mobile hairdresser. Which thrilled me, not only because it showed she was thinking about a future, but a future that she was confident would include Roman.

In the meantime, however, she had other plans. 'I've been thinking,' she said to me when she got home from her unit one afternoon, 'that I need to spend more time with Riley.' It was just a week after the miscarriage and I'd taken her round to see her twice, and she'd clearly been mulling things over.

'Ri-ight,' I said, anticipating there was still more to come. 'And?' I patted the sofa, beckoning her to come and sit with me.

'And I was thinking that, just for the moment, I need to be spending less time at school and more time helping her out. Not stopping school, exactly –' she was quick to reassure me. 'Just going in a bit less so I can be there to help Riley in the daytime. Like taking the boys to school and picking them up for her. I could do that for her next week, at least, couldn't I? I mean, she's still supposed to be taking it easy' – she was impressively well informed – 'and David's got work, and it would be a big help to them, wouldn't it, if I did that?'

I resisted the urge to point out that these were all things I'd done before, was still doing and would continue to do, as long as was necessary, because that was of no consequence. She was so anxious to help out, bless her. And why shouldn't she? 'And then there's the cleaning,' she went on, causing me to blink back my surprise. 'I could go round and do that for her, couldn't I? Help keep the place straight. And it would be company for her, wouldn't it? Take her mind off things.'

I agreed that it would. And that perhaps I could have a word with the head at the unit and explain that, for at least a couple of weeks, she'd be in rather less. Frankly, the whole thing was a revelation. She seemed so grown up, all of a sudden, as if overnight someone had come in and swapped the demanding teenager for a more sensible girl, much older than her years. And it was irrelevant that this might well be as much about her own loss as Riley's. What mattered was that she wanted to help and that she felt Riley's pain. That was what counted. I reached out and gave her a big hug.

'That's so kind of you, love, but you know, you don't have to do all that. You've got school and your friends to see and, well, you'll want to make the most of having fun with your mates while you can, won't you? And' – I paused, unsure whether to broach it – 'you're still hurting too – hurting for Roman – and you need time to get yourself together too.'

Roman was very much the elephant in the room. Emma had been twice to see him now, at the same family centre she'd visited with Tarim, and on both occasions had come home pale and drawn and uncommunicative. It was the one area in which even Riley couldn't make headway, Emma telling her, as well as me, that it was something she just didn't want to talk about. That she'd feel better if she didn't. It was the proverbial closed book. We had to respect that, obviously, but I hated to see this outwardly functional, mostly chirpy teenager keeping so much hurt locked inside her, out of reach.

But then I hadn't had her upbringing, had I? Perhaps that was a defence mechanism that worked for her – perhaps she was right to keep Roman in a tightly closed emotional box. She had probably spent most of her life doing that, in any case, the pain of her mother's repeated rejections being a definite case in point. She hardly spoke of her, and that was fine – again, she must deal with things her own way. And perhaps this was the same; only when and if she knew she could allow herself to believe they might be reunited would she allow herself to share how she felt.

She shook her head now. 'You're wrong, Casey,' she said, and she looked like she meant it. 'This isn't about me, this is about Riley. She was there for me when I felt like there was no point going on, and now I want to be there for her.'

All the same, I felt I'd better run Emma's ideas past Riley first. In my enthusiasm for encouraging Emma's emotional development, I didn't want to add to her misery by forcing Emma's pregnancy in her face. While Emma was out with Tash for a bit, after tea I phoned Riley to run it by her – explain what Emma wanted to do, and share my reservations.

'Oh, Mum, don't think like that,' she said. 'You really mustn't. Yes, I feel like I've been hit by a truck, and yes, I do keep feeling teary, but it's like the doctors said – these things happen to women everywhere, all the time, and I'm lucky. I already have a family to cherish, so I've no business moping and feeling sorry for myself. Well, a bit sorry for myself' – she laughed, and my heart really went out to her – 'but not for too long, and Emma will be the best tonic imaginable. I'm not going to sit there distraught because she's having her baby and I'm not. And, actually, she's right. She will be a great distraction, and, you know what, I like her. She's a sweetheart. She's been to hell and back and she's there worrying about cleaning my skirting boards? Bring it on – she is my kind of gal.'

So Riley and Emma had spoken and I was only too happy to listen. No matter that their combined ages didn't even add up to my one, their combined wisdom belied their tender years, and over the next couple of weeks I could see the benefits in both of them, with Riley taking on the mantle of Emma's pregnancy guru – demanding to know her vegetable intake and whether she was getting sufficient exercise, and Emma parrying by giggling and pointing out that she didn't need any more exercise than she was getting by scrubbing filthy football-boot marks off Riley's kitchen floor.

It was a tonic for all of us and we'd frequently be reduced to fits of the giggles as if, having rediscovered laughing, we couldn't work out how to stop.

And I was to see another heartening development just a few days later, when I asked her about celebrating her fifteenth birthday. It seemed hardly possible that she had been with us almost a year now, yet she had. And she was finally that magical 'fifteen' she'd been so keen to tell us she 'nearly was' for much of the last six months.

But Emma didn't want to celebrate her birthday.

'It doesn't feel right to,' she said when I suggested we do something – even if just a quiet family dinner. 'What with Riley losing her baby, and me losing Roman. It just doesn't feel right to. You don't mind, do you?'

I was so touched. And also saddened, when she went on to explain that she didn't set much store by birthdays anyway.

'I got used to it,' she said, 'because Mum only remembered half the time anyway. One year it would be, like, nothing, because she'd be out of it and couldn't care less, then one time she would remember, or she'd remember it the wrong month or something and she'd like buy me shed loads of rubbish that I didn't even want and we'd have no money for the electric or food and stuff. No,' she said, 'let's not. Let's just concentrate on Riley. I mean it would be nice to get a few bits from Primark or something – actually, I'd really like that because none of my skinny jeans fit me – but, nah. Let's not bother. Not this year.'

It was all I could do not to weep right there in front of her. And give thanks that whatever her mum was or wasn't, with her multiple rejections, her capriciousness, her unpredictability, 'not around' was a state of affairs that suited me – and Emma's precious emotional health – just fine.

* * *

There was still one particularly persistent fly in the ointment, however – one I realised I'd forgotten about only when the house phone rang one evening, and when Mike went into the hall and answered it, he followed up by saying, 'Hello, Billy.'

It took a second or two for me to work out who Billy was, but Emma was all ears in an instant. 'Tarim's dad,' she mouthed at me as we sat and waited for what might be coming next. I picked up the remote and lowered the soap opera we'd all been glued to, the better to hear. I hoped this wasn't about to become one as well.

'No, I'm sorry, she can't,' we heard him say. There was a pause while Billy spoke again. 'Because I don't think it's a good idea,' Mike said, 'that's why.' And then another. And then 'Hang on.'

There was another pause and next thing Mike was in the living-room doorway. 'Love, it's Tarim's dad,' he said. 'Says he wants to speak to you. You don't have to. But I said I'd ask –'

I glanced at Emma, willing her to tell him where to go. She wouldn't cave in now, would she? Please not. Not now. But I needn't have worried. Emma was already shaking her head. 'No, Mike. I don't want to speak to him, thank you. I don't ever want to speak to him,' she added, chin tipped up. 'That's it.'

Mike winked at her and walked back into the hall. 'Well, that's up to you,' we heard him say. 'But that's something you'll have to speak to social services about. It's up to them now … No, it doesn't involve Emma. Not at all. Roman's in care … yes, that's right. You'll need to call them. It's really nothing to do with us now …'

When he came back we were both poised to hear the details of the rest of it. There was no raised voice, but that didn't mean there was no potential for trouble. Putting two and two together, it seemed they wanted access to Roman. Which was rich given that the last time we'd had dealings with Tarim he'd been mouthing off about how he was disowning them all.

Mike confirmed it. 'They're after contact,' he said. 'Want to know how Tarim can get to see Roman.'

Emma looked horrified. 'They won't actually let him do that, will they?'

I didn't know what to say to her. In fact, all things being equal, they couldn't not. With Tarim confirmed as the father, they had no grounds to refuse him contact, provided he kept his nose clean. As a child in care, Roman had as much right to contact with his father as he did his mother, who was looking at me now, open mouthed.

'I don't know for sure, love,' I answered truthfully, 'but even if they do decide to allow it, one thing I do know is that it would be supervised – no question of that – and that he'll have a long way to go before they put anything in place anyway – even a short visit at the family centre.'

She looked even more anxious. 'What, with me?' she squeaked. 'He'd be allowed to just come and join in?'

I shook my head. 'Heavens no. You never have to see him again, ever, love. Don't worry about that. No, it would be entirely separate.' I squeezed her arm. 'Don't worry.'

'Has he been in touch with you about this already, love?' Mike asked as he sat down again. 'Funny them calling us on the house phone.'

'No, not at all,' she said. 'He couldn't, 'cos I blocked his number yonks ago. I know he was bothering Tash for a bit, but she blocked him as well in the end. So that's probably why. God, I wish he'd just sod off and leave us alone.' Then she blushed. 'Sorry. But, I do, I really do wish he'd go away. Find some other girl – I wish I'd see that. Wish I'd see him with another girl, 'cos then I'd know he'd finally decided to let me go.'

For myself, I decided wishing wasn't quite good enough. So the next day I called John so I could establish more in the way of facts. If Tarim was serious about shaping up and being a father to Roman, so be it. Every child deserved the love of the people that made them – that was never a bad thing. And the first image I ever had of Tarim was also a very powerful one. No one was black and white and, however corrosive and aggressive his relationship with Emma, it was not for me to decide he should have no role in his infant son's life. But, tender though the moments with his son had been to witness, I had a hunch that this was perhaps more about Emma than about Roman. It was a thought that had taken root as soon as she'd told us that she'd blocked Tarim from calling her mobile.

And John confirmed it. 'Oh, I know all about this, Casey – in fact it was one of the things that was on the agenda for the progress meeting we've scheduled with you next week.

Sorry you've been bothered. Was he bothersome?'

'No,' I said. 'It was actually his father who made the phone call on his behalf. Though he was there –'

'That doesn't surprise me. I get the impression from Maggie that his dad's a bit of a pawn in this whole game. The truth is that he seems genuine. Keen to get his son straightened out. But so far, though they've made all the right noises and filled the forms in, there've been two meetings arranged for Tarim to come in and discuss things, neither of which he's bothered to show up for.'

'So my hunch might be right. He's just using Roman to try and get to Emma.'

'Nail on the head, I think. And he wouldn't be the last man to do that sort of thing, would he?'

We both chuckled. 'No, he wouldn't,' I agreed.

'And she's standing firm as far as he's concerned?'

'Firm as anything,' I reported happily.

'So far so good, then,' John said. 'And it's been far as well, hasn't it?'

It had indeed. All things considered, we'd come a long way already. There was just the small detail that we still had a long way to go.

Chapter 20

It had been a curiously quiet end to an eventful and trau-matic year. With Roman's first birthday having come and gone, and Emma's passing largely unremarked, the usual fairy-light fest that was the Watson family Christmas passed in equally understated style. Which wasn't to say that we didn't have some fun – we were all together, we had some snow, everyone ate their body weight in nuts and chocolate. But Roman's absence, along with the baby daughter Riley had lost, cast a slight shadow over things; how could it not? Though, for all that, as Christmases went, this was a good one for Emma. She'd told me it was one of the few proper family Christmases she had ever been a part of in her young life. Her first with us had been a blur, obviously, but this last one had been a gift. 'It's the first time,' she confided to me, 'that I've felt like it was proper. Like the Christmas stuff you see on the telly.' She went on to tell me that hers more often than not began alone, in their flat, because her mum had to go to the pub before lunch on Christmas day, because it was the one day they closed after lunch. She had only the foggiest memories of any 'Christmassy sort of Christmas' – a blurry image of a tinsel tree and presents arranged around it, a dim recollection of a grandmother she could hardly remember, talk of a granddad who was already gone.

My heart went out to her and I was thankful that Roman was still so tiny. Was I unrealistic to hope that this would be the last Christmas he had to spend without his mummy? I truly hoped not.

Emma had been particularly taken with, and, to an extent, awed by Justin the second time she met him. He was now living in supported lodgings and working hard as a council gardener – he was now almost an adult and nearly as tall as Kieron. And when I explained about Justin's background – how he'd been passed from pillar to post in the care system from the age of just five, after having been abandoned by his heroin-addicted mother – I think it really brought Emma up short. It certainly gave her pause for thought. Serious thought, too, about just how determined she was to do what she had to do to get her little boy back with her again.

Not that Roman wasn't thriving – he was. Well, I presumed he was from the pictures. I'd actually been asked if I wanted to go and see him, more than once, but I'd chickened out, still feeling too delicate to trust myself. I felt daft as a brush admitting it, but I missed Roman more than I let on to anyone outside the family, and the last thing I wanted was to see him and blubber and have him get all upset by being visited by some bonkers old lady.

It was February now, one of the coldest I could remember in a long time. Not the best time, perhaps, for a new life to enter the world, but mother nature was no respecter of schedules. Or, indeed, sleep.

'Casey, Casey … wake up. Wake *up* … I think it's started!'

The sound came to me as part of the most bizarre dream. I was in a caravan park, somewhere seasidey but, instead of the usual sand, sea and sun combo, the whole resort seemed to be made out of fruit. Instead of palm trees there were upside-down clumps of giant bananas, and the deck chairs were slices of melon. And most weirdly, we'd gone on holiday – me and Mike, all the family – and, for some reason, we'd taken a small Shetland pony. Which, for reasons that escaped me, we had decided had better join us in the caravan, so I'd made it up a bed in the living room. I'd never had a Shetland pony – though the kids had certainly talked me into having all sorts of smaller pets as children – and as I struggled to work out where I was, not to mention why, all I could think of was how important it was, before I went off to see who was calling from outside the caravan, that the pony didn't put its backside through any of the windows.

Something was tugging at me now, as well. Was it the flipping pony again, trying to bite me? It was only when I realised that it had spoken rather than neighed that it suddenly hit me this wasn't real. I was actually lying in the dark, somewhere, having been jolted into consciousness, and there was a mouth talking at me, right by my face.

A human mouth. My eyes snapped fully open. 'Jesus!' I jabbered, rubbing my eyes as they began to adjust to the darkness. 'Emma! God, I'm so sorry! Are you okay?'

She didn't look okay, that was for sure.

She shook her head. 'Nooooo,' she sobbed. 'I'm not. I've got these God-awful cramps keep coming. I can't sleep, it hurts so much. I think it's the baby coming, Casey.'

She was just over a week before her due date, so I knew it could well be. And there was no doubt she looked like she was ready to have one. Having not seen her carrying Roman, I didn't actually have a yardstick, but in the last four weeks or so she had ballooned up to what felt like twice her usual size. And that's when it hit me why the dream had come about. The fruit – yes! She'd been wolfing down kilos of the stuff lately. And only last night she'd been on hands and knees, rocking back and forth, in the living room, resting her pelvis while I sat and watched *EastEnders*. And I'd told her that with her hair hanging down like a mane she looked like she was our pet Shetland pony. 'Uuuurghhh,' she started moaning then, albeit trying to do it quietly, so as not to disturb Mike, bless her heart.

I pinged the light on. 'Mike!' I said, shaking him awake roughly. This was no time for sleeping. We had somewhere to *be*. I knew just how much of a hurry second babies could be in, too. 'Mike!' I said again, as he groaned and rolled over. 'Spit spot! We have a labour on our hands!'

'*Am* I in labour, d'you think, Casey?' Emma just about managed to gasp, as the contraction she'd obviously had started dying down. '*Really?* I mean, it feels like I am … oh, but I can't *bear* to think I'm not. What if we get there and I'm not and they send us home again and then it starts again and … uurrgghh … I have to go through this for, like, *ever*?'

Mike had darted into the bathroom to throw some clothes on, in the interests of decency, since Emma had plopped herself on our bed and now couldn't move. 'Calm down,' I said. '*Breathe*. Yes, I'm sure you're probably in labour.' Which was a contradiction in terms, but no matter. There was no way I was going to adopt a 'wait and see' approach here. I knew how quickly these things could progress. I felt her brow, which was clammy, and checked the time on the bedside clock. 'Let's see how soon the next pain comes, then we'll have an idea, okay? And in the meantime' – I was running around her now, trying to get myself out of my pyjamas – 'we'll get ourselves organised to –'

I stopped mid-utterance. Emma had leapt up – well, as far as she could leap anywhere – and was emitting a different sound now, a sort of 'ohhhhh!'

'What's the matter?' I said, but soon realised I already had my answer. Her waters had broken – and had only narrowly missed our bed.

'Don't worry about that,' I chided, as Emma looked aghast at the pool of liquid darkening the bedside rug beneath her bare feet. 'Just hang on there. I'll go and get you some fresh trackie bottoms to change into. And your slippers and dressing gown, and your bag. Mike! Come on! What are you doing in there? We need to go now!'

'And my phone. Don't forget my phone!' Emma shouted after me as I flew across the landing. I rolled my eyes. Ever the teenager, even now.

When Emma had asked me if I'd be her birth partner I had had two principal emotions. The first was joy. I was so touched that she wanted me there to hold her hand, I really was, because it meant such a lot to me about what we'd achieved. That she could trust me to be there during this most intimate of life events spoke volumes about the bond we'd finally forged.

But at the same time I did feel just a tiny bit squeamish. I could roll my sleeves up and get on with most icky things – I'd been doing that for years, and I'd been present at the births of both Levi and Jackson. Which had been an enormous privilege, because seeing a baby come into the world is a privilege like no other. It was just that this felt slightly different. Should it be me? Was it the right thing? I wasn't sure.

But when I asked Emma if she was sure she had come back immediately. 'Casey, you *have* to – I can't do it without you. And who else would it be if not you? You're the closest thing to a mother I've ever had in my whole life. And don't you *want* to be there?' She'd looked so anxious when she'd said that. 'Don't you think it would just be *so* wicked, like, when she's older and you can tell her, "I was there when you were born"?'

And there was something else. Even as I was telling her that it was okay, that I *would* be there, she was already telling me the other reason she'd asked me to be her birth partner. 'I don't think I can bear being on my own again, I really can't.'

Which was the clincher. The thought that when she gave birth to Roman she didn't have a soul to support her. So we must. That was the main thing that Mike and I did, above everything – be there for the kids we looked after. We might never see some of them ever again, obviously. Some moved on, moved away, left their troubled pasts behind them, and in these cases that was exactly how it should be. But in other cases these relationships had and would always endure. And this was clearly one such. In as much as you could predict anything that happened in the future, this little girl – and to me she was still very much a little girl – would stay in our lives, hopefully, as well as our hearts.

I ran into Emma's bedroom and gathered up everything I thought we needed: the fresh trackie bottoms, a loose top, her slippers, her fleecy dressing gown, the phone – God help me if I forgot to bring her mobile – *and* the charger. And, finally, the baby bag we'd prepared a week earlier. We had plenty of kit, because we still had lots of the things we'd brought for Roman, as well as the paraphernalia she'd arrived with all that time ago. I'd got everything out ready, too – ever the organiser, me – and now all that remained was to see this new life into the world. As I took a last glance around Emma's bedroom, I felt a shiver of anticipation. All being well, by this time tomorrow we'd have a brand new little girl sleeping here.

I went back into our bedroom then, where Emma was still sitting on the bed, panting. I could see she was trying to take heed of all the antenatal advice and breathe through it, but I could also see she was beginning to struggle. I'd been out of the room for only a couple of minutes and if she was already in the middle of her next contraction, then this baby wouldn't be hanging about.

'Come on, love,' I said, as I heard Mike moving about downstairs, finding keys, opening the front door. 'Let's get you into these clean things and get you downstairs.'

'I don't know if I can stand up,' she told me, her voice querulous. 'It feels like everything might fall out!'

'I know, love,' I said, helping her into a standing position anyway. 'But it won't – not yet, I promise you. Come on now,' I said, getting hold of the waistband of her wet trackies. 'And excuse the invasion of your privacy, but let's get these wet things off and get you changed.'

The contraction having subsided, it didn't take long to get Emma ready. And once she had her slippers and dressing gown on over the top as well, I helped her down to the waiting car and bundled her quickly in.

The drive to the hospital was really traumatic. Because there was no way she could sit, I'd had to let Emma have the back seat to herself, and almost as soon as we left the contractions became relentless so she spent the entire journey on her back with her legs in the air, screaming like a banshee at every massive wave of pain. I felt for her. There isn't a mum alive who doesn't know what that feels like – and I winced along, empathising madly. She also had a vice-like grip on my hand which hurt like the devil, since it was the one with my rings on and they dug in. And poor Mike – our trusty driver – didn't escape the drama either. Every time she screamed he slowed down a bit, thinking it might help a little. But of course it didn't. 'For God's sake, Mike,' I shrieked above the noise, 'put your flipping foot down! We've got to get there – like NOW!' And, 'Do you want her to give birth in an elderly, clapped-out and frankly grubby Vauxhall Astra? *Do* you? Well I don't. Drive faster!'

Which, of course, made Emma panic all the more, and scream correspondingly louder. 'Oh my fucking GOD!' she screeched. 'I think I'm dying, Casey. I really do! Oh my God, oh my God – make it *stop*!'

Once at the hospital, which happened not a moment too soon, it was like a scene from some macabre black comedy. Mike and I had to practically drag Emma from the back seat, as if she was a particularly heavy and unwieldy rolled-up rug. She was panting now and starting to groan and bear down and for a moment or two it was if she was superglued to the car. 'I can't!' she puffed as, one arm around my shoulder while Mike held the wheelchair, I tried to prise her fingers from the car door-frame. I eventually freed them, but this set up another bout of banshee wailing. 'It's too late!' she kept crying as we bundled her into the wheelchair and through the double doors. 'Oh my God, the baby's coming! It's co-uurrgghh! – it's coming!' – much to the amusement of the night porter we passed.

Eventually – and with the baby still in place, rather than on the lino – we made it through admissions and up to the delivery suite. But if I thought there might be a calm before the storm so soon to come now, I was very much mistaken. There's a saying that has always made me bristle. It's the 'You can take the girl out of the estate but you can't take the estate out of the girl' and I've always thought it really derogatory. I was an estate girl myself – it's where I grew up and I'm not ashamed of it. I also hated the implication that if you were brought up in such a place, then you were rougher than your more well-off peers.

Which is nonsense, but that night even I found myself shocked at some of the language that came out of Emma's mouth. Even the bluest comedian, as Mike observed when we stepped out for a breather, would have been red in the face.

'Get this fucking thing out of me NOW!' was about the mildest imprecation that came out of Emma's rosebud lips as she set about the business of delivering what looked like being a very big baby from her teeny, skinny fifteen-year-old frame. And needless to say, when Emma commanded 'Don't move me, bitch!' the midwife she addressed wasn't too impressed. Like the night porter, she'd obviously seen pretty much everything, and everyone knows that mums-to-be don't often have the best track record, particularly when sucking on gas and air. But it was obvious, even though nothing was actually said, that she thought Emma the most potty-mouthed of spoilt, toxic teenagers and us a pair of pathetic over-liberal parents.

But there was no time to dwell. There was a baby at the centre of this, and I knew that the minute she made her appearance, everything – just everything – would be fine again. I felt for Emma's camera in my pocket, happy to wrap my hand around it. And I'd capture the moment myself.

Mercedes Shelley Tasha came into the world at 7.15 on a freezing February morning, weighing in at a respectable 7lb 3oz, kicking and screaming like a banshee, very much her mother's daughter. As for me, well, as per the plan, I was at the pushing end, of course. While Mike patrolled the corridor and took tea with the night shift at the nurses' station, I had the privilege of seeing her take her first gasping breath. And I was surprised to find myself crying every bit as hard as when my own precious grandsons were born. And then laughing because seeing a junior midwife munching on a banana made me realise that for the rest of my life that connection would endure. A mad dream about fruit and Shetland ponies in caravans and the birth of this gorgeous baby girl.

I praised Emma to the hilt for being so brave and strong and clever, because it really did feel as if this way-too-young mother had achieved something no other woman ever had. It was a beautiful moment and I was very, very proud of her.

'Oh, my, Emma, she is just such a cutie,' I told her, while, blessed with a first hold after her mum, I cradled the tiny new life in my arms. Emma, by now, was busy texting Tash to let her know she'd given Mercedes her name.

'Does she look like me, d'you think?' she wanted to know. 'You know, even a bit?'

She had black hair, deep olive skin and those huge blue-black baby eyes. To a casual observer she looked very much her father's daughter. But to me? No. Yes, he was in there, of course. But what I could also see, so clearly, was that certain unique something that's difficult to pin down unless you know the mum really well: the tilt of the chin, the set of the mouth, the way her eyebrows arched ironically, the way her button nose sat on her face so prettily, so just *so* … Yes, I thought, *you*, little lady, are going to be your mother's daughter. You are going to defy the odds, and make a brilliant and happy life, despite your less than auspicious start. You're going to be just like your mum, you are, I thought – you're going to be okay. Despite everything, you're going to be *fine*.

I gulped back a tear, because I believed it now as well. 'Oh, goodness, *yes*, love. She looks *just* like you,' I said.

Epilogue

Emma did indeed bring Mercedes home the following day, and, right from that moment, everything really did seem different. She was as besotted as it was possible for a mother to be and, with the crucial addition of confidence in her armoury, took to the business of caring for her newborn infant like a duck to the proverbial water.

She was also strong and fit and bursting with energy, and I recall thinking more than once that while no one would ever wish two children on a girl who was still no more than a child herself, from a physical perspective she was actually in her prime. All that healthy eating that Riley had forced her to do was obviously making its presence felt. As I was able to tell John honestly when he called round a week later, I had barely had to lift a finger.

But for all the joy of those early days there was still much to be resolved. Emma still had a lot of hurdles to climb over and hoops to jump through before she would be at the place she wanted to be – independently raising both her kids. In the short term she had to once again persuade Hannah (once again on her twice-weekly visiting schedule) that she had got to grips with the responsibility she had on her young shoulders, and accept that while there were all sorts of extenuating circumstances (her inability to extricate herself from Tarim's influence, and her deprived and difficult childhood) when it came to the welfare of her little ones excuses counted for nothing. If she wanted to keep Mercedes, she had to continue the good work she'd been doing for the later months of her pregnancy – putting the child's welfare at the forefront of her mind at all times. There was a greater mountain to climb as far as Roman was concerned, obviously, as now he was settled with a long-term foster family it would be up to Emma to prove that she could not only cope with her infant daughter as a single mum, but that she could also provide a fit home for her little boy as well. And as every parent knows, two children are a lot more to deal with than one, particularly when one of them is a toddler.

But I had faith in her. And it wasn't blind faith, either. I was to find out just how far Emma had come emotionally when, only a month into Mercedes' life, a complication reared its head, in the form of contact, out of the blue, from her own mother.

It came in the form of a letter, sent to social services and passed on to John, who phoned to impart the news and sound me out on how Emma might react. And it was a shock. Emma had not heard a thing from her since receiving that cruel, distressing letter, and, if that were a measure of what the poor girl could expect, I was very glad that state of affairs had endured.

She had phoned as well, apparently following up on what she'd written, and was keen to find out if Emma would see her.

'Says she's made great progress,' John told me. 'Hang on, let me read the letter to you. Right, here we are … finished my programme – that'll be some sort of rehab, then, I'm guessing – let me see … lots of meetings … been clean for four months now … got my life together … blah blah blah, blah blah blah – ah, yes, here it is. "So though I know it's a big ask, I was wondering if you could speak to Emma on my behalf and pass on the enclosed letter. I realise that last time I communicated with her I was in a bad place – and a terrible state – and said lots of hurtful, cruel, unforgivable things, but I am really trying this time – trying to change my life, truly. And it hurts so much that I have hurt and alienated the only thing that was precious to me. I know it's a long shot but I really do want to make amends to my daughter and I would also love to meet my new granddaughter." So that's about the size of it,' John finished. 'So, what do you think? How d'you think she'll take it?'

I was shocked – I hadn't given Emma's mum a thought in so long. Well, except in as much as she passed though my mind as a negative factor in Emma's life. And my first reaction was, I'll admit, that she'd be better off having nothing more to do with her – after all, this getting clean and then falling off the wagon again cycle had been one that had been repeated many times.

But two things altered my view. The first was that I examined my own feelings. I recalled how sad I'd been when my own beloved daughter had lost her baby, and how much it had meant to me – someone with no familial connection to Emma – to have been there to watch that very grandchild come into the world. The second was Emma herself. Who was I to try and influence her about her mother? And it was a lesson I was to learn at first hand.

When I told Emma about the letter John would be delivering from her mother, she rolled her eyes. 'Well, we'll wait and see,' she said, sounding every inch the mother in the equation, with her own mother the unreliable child. And when it came, and she sat there and read it – which she did right in front of me as soon as it was given to her – she read through silently, thoughtfully, re-reading sections here and there, and only then, when she was done, did she look up or comment.

'You might think it's mad,' she said, 'but you know what, she actually wants to come and see us –'

'What's mad about that?' I said. 'If I were her I'd definitely want to see you both.'

'That's not the mad bit,' she said, giving me a sheepish little grin. 'The mad bit is that I'd really, really like that.'

I was a bit taken aback that she thought I'd feel anything but joy that she should say that, but then, once I thought about it, I realised that she must have had years of people banging on to her about not wasting her energy and hopes and time on a mother who let her down so much – perhaps so much that she actually felt reluctant to confess the obvious: that she still loved her mother, because that's what children were programmed from birth to do. God knew, I'd seen enough of it – kids who'd been abused and mistreated in ways that were barely even thinkable, let alone printable, and yet they doggedly went on loving them just the same.

'I think that's absolutely lovely,' I said to her, hugging her. 'And very generous of you to be so forgiving – that you're willing to give her another chance after everything that's gone before.'

And then I learned the first lesson. 'How could I not, Casey?' she said quietly. 'I've been thinking lots. About how much time I've felt being just so bloody hurt and miserable – and angry. I've been *so* angry. I think about it so much – and I sometimes wonder if the whole reason I stayed with Tarim was just to get back at my mum because I was just so, so *angry* with her about everything.

'And then there's Roman. And I keep thinking just how much I messed things up for him, and how much I want him back with me and Mercedes and how wrong it all is. And I think how he might feel about me and what a shit mother I've been to him –'

'That's not true, love,' I said gently.

'Yes it is – to *him* it is, Casey. He should be with me. I should be taking care of him, and I'm not. He's been taken off to strangers. That's not right, is it? However good they are at taking care of him. And just imagine if he was older and, like, thought about how I'd messed up things with him. And decided he would give me a second chance? *That's* why I have to.'

So Emma's mum Shelley came and visited, and she was almost exactly as I'd imagined her: slight, and if a little worn down by the life she'd led, a lot like Emma. Perhaps older than I expected – I recalled the grandparents being elderly, so that figured – but mostly just a sad woman trying to make everything better. Well, as much as she could under the circumstances, anyway.

And Emma handled everything brilliantly. She told her mum that she intended to fight to get Roman back, and when Shelley told her that she'd be happy to do anything she could to help that happen Emma merely smiled politely and said, 'That's kind, Mum, but I can do this one on my own, thanks.' And when she left and I put my arms around Emma and told her she'd done really well, making things up with her mum, she just grinned and said, 'Yeah, but you can see what she's like now, can't you?'

'In what way?' I'd asked her, not quite understanding where this was leading.

She pulled a face. 'Casey, she's a flake! You could surely see that, couldn't you? So don't you worry that I'm going to bomb off and set up home with her. No chance of that happening. Don't worry.'

But the love was there, and however breezy Emma's demeanour following the meeting I still felt the need to counsel caution where her heart and hopes were concerned.

And it was at that point that I *knew* that Emma would manage to break the cycle, because when I tried to do just that – counsel her about not getting her hopes up about her mother's sobriety – she had so much wisdom, in her small way, to impart.

There would be no past or future where Emma's mother was concerned, clearly. No promises of happy ever afters that both knew one of them would have difficulty coming good on, and no days ruined by admonishments about past misdemeanours either.

'I'm just going to take it for what it is,' she told me. 'Forgive and forget and see what happens. If she's there she's there, if she isn't she isn't. I have my own kids to concentrate on now.'

And concentrate she did. As soon as it became clear to Hannah and Maggie that Emma's desire to get Roman back was serious, the whole assessment process was ramped up once again. There had been no further contact from Tarim (for which I, at least, was very thankful) so it was now a question of Emma being encouraged to think about what could be done in order to make a case for Roman's care order being revoked. And it was a process that Mike and I weren't involved in. We'd agreed to keep Emma till she was sixteen, but that had been before realising she was pregnant, and it was clear to me that the prospect of going through the same process with Mercedes as we had with Roman simply wasn't going to work. Much as I wanted to be there for this fledgling little family – we all did – I knew that it had to be under a different sort of arrangement. We had to move towards Emma getting her own place with Mercedes, getting settled, thinking about her studies and, most importantly, work. In short, if she was to get Roman home she first had to prove beyond doubt that she had created a home for him to go to.

And that suited me. The thought of falling in love with another baby that wasn't mine was something I knew I couldn't even think about right now. And, luckily, Emma had already made some decisions in that regard. While she could, in the short term, go on to another mother and baby placement, she was much more keen on the idea of getting on with her life, and moving into a small supported unit of the kind Tash had been in since day one.

Social services found one quickly, as well. It was a perfect set-up, too – she'd be one of four young mums, all with their babies. And all independent, in that they each had their own little flat, but with the support of a manager 24/7.

'And they all have just one,' Hannah told her, passing Emma the leaflet. 'So you'd have the biggest flat, since you'll be the only one with two.'

Emma's eyes became saucers. 'Does that mean –' she began.

Maggie exchanged a look with Hannah, but her eyes were still twinkling. 'Not *just* yet,' she said. 'Hold your horses. But we thought we'd better plan ahead, didn't we, Hannah, and, well, if things continue as they are, when you move in you'll be able to have Roman over for visits, and then for sleepovers and, well, we can go from there, can't we?'

You could almost taste the joy in the room.

So that's what happened. On a warm early summer's day, four months after Mercedes' birth, the little family, not quite complete yet, but well on the way to being so, left our home to take their first steps towards a new and better life. And with everything in place to ensure they had the best chance of making it, as well. They'd have Maggie and Hannah on hand, a specialist key worker as well, fellow mums to provide companionship and round-the-clock support. And with all that in place Emma could and would return to education, working to get qualifications in both English and Maths. After that, it was her hope to get on that hairdressing course at college, so she could one day provide for her little ones without help.

And with us in the background, a phone call or a visit away, as needed, and with the firm arrangement that while Emma went back to school I'd be the one who looked after Mercedes. And, in time, I'm so pleased to report, Roman too. And, no, he hadn't quite forgotten who I was.

Another year on, and Emma's life has changed beyond all recognition. She got her GCSEs in English and Maths and did manage to secure a place in a further education college, where she met a nice boy called Jordan. And as well as a fledgling new relationship, she also managed to get a job, the salon where she did day release offering her a full apprenticeship just a short while after her sixteenth birthday. She and Jordan now have their own flat, complete with Roman and little Mercedes and, periodically, whenever she's on form enough to come and see them, Shelley – who always visits laden down with presents.

Jordan is a sweetheart; two years older than Emma, and very sensible and grounded, he works in a local engineering factory. They both work incredibly hard, so we're always happy to play foster nan and granddad to Roman and Mercedes, so they can enjoy the odd well-deserved night out. As far as the future goes, well, who knows what will happen? That's the thing about the future, isn't it? No one can say. All *I* can say is that, for the moment, they're all well and happy, and if you can say anything in life, that's probably the most important.

As for me, I'm happy too. And a gran again, to boot, Riley having become pregnant again shortly after Emma moved into her unit. And, yes, to her delight, she had a 'pink' one.

CASEY WATSON

One woman determined to
make a difference.

Read Casey's poignant
memoirs and be inspired.

Five-year-old Justin was desperate and helpless

Six years after being taken into care, Justin has had 20 failed placements. Casey and her family are his last hope.

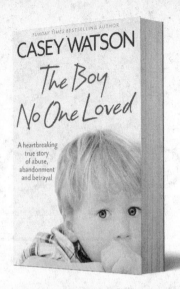

THE BOY NO ONE LOVED

A damaged girl haunted by her past

Sophia pushes Casey to the limits, threatening the safety of the whole family. Can Casey make a difference in time?

CRYING FOR HELP

Abused siblings who do not know what it means to be loved

With new-found security and trust, Casey helps Ashton and Olivia to rebuild their lives.

LITTLE PRISONERS

Branded 'vicious and evil', eight-year-old Spencer asks to be taken into care

Casey and her family are disgusted: kids aren't born evil. Despite the challenges Spencer brings, they are determined to help him find a loving home.

TOO HURT TO STAY

A young girl secretly caring for her mother

Abigail has been dealing with pressures no child should face. Casey has the difficult challenge of helping her to learn to let go.

MOMMY'S LITTLE HELPER

Two boys with an unlikely bond

With Georgie and Jenson, Casey is facing her toughest test yet.

BREAKING THE SILENCE

A teenage mother and baby in need of a loving home

At fourteen, Emma is just a child herself – and one who's never been properly mothered.

A LAST KISS FOR MOMMY

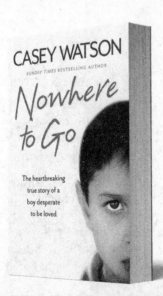

Eleven-year-old Tyler has stabbed his stepmother and has nowhere to go

With his birth mother dead and a father who doesn't want him, what can be done to stop his young life spiralling out of control?

NOWHERE TO GO

What is the secret behind Imogen's silence?

Discover the shocking and devastating past of a child with severe behavioural problems.

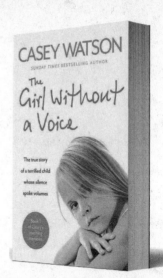

THE GIRL WITHOUT A VOICE

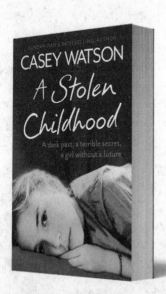

Kiara appears tired and distressed, and the school wants Casey to take her under her wing for a while

On the surface, everything points to a child who is upset that her parents have separated. The horrific truth, however, shocks Casey to the core.

A STOLEN CHILDHOOD

Flip is being raised by her alcoholic mother, and comes to Casey after a fire at their home

Flip has Foetal Alcohol Syndrome (FAS), but it soon turns out that this is just the tip of the iceberg . . .

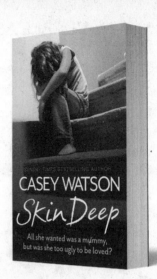

SKIN DEEP

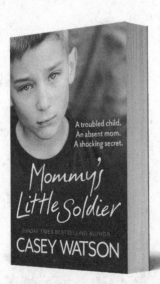

Leo isn't a bad lad, but his frequent absences from school mean he's on the brink of permanent exclusion

Leo is clearly hiding something, and Casey knows that if he is to have any kind of future, it's up to her to find out the truth.

MOMMY'S LITTLE SOLDIER

AVAILABLE AS E-BOOK ONLY

Cameron is a sweet boy who seems happy in his skin – making him rather different from most of the other children Casey has cared for

But what happens when Cameron disappears? Will Casey's worst fears be realised?

JUST A BOY

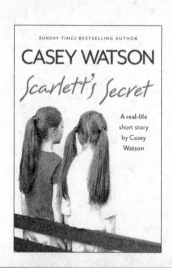

Jade and Scarlett, seventeen-year-old twins, share a terrible secret

Can Casey help them come to terms with the truth and rediscover their sibling connection?

SCARLETT'S SECRET

Nathan has a sometime alter ego called Jenny who is the only one who knows the secrets of his disturbed past

But where is Jenny when she is most needed?

NO PLACE FOR NATHAN

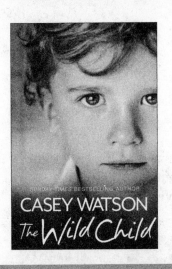

Angry and hurting, eight-year-old Connor is from a broken home

As streetwise as they come, he's determined to cause trouble. But Casey is convinced there is a frightened child beneath the swagger.

THE WILD CHILD

FEEL HEART.
FEEL HOPE.
READ CASEY.

Discover more about Casey Watson.
Visit www.caseywatson.co.uk

Find Casey Watson on &